PAPER
BACK
LYRICS

COMPLETE LYRICS FOR
OVER 135 SONGS

The

1990s

HAL•LEONARD®

ISBN-13: 978-1-4234-1196-3
ISBN-10: 1-4234-1196-X

HAL•LEONARD®
CORPORATION
7777 W. BLUEMOUND RD. P.O. BOX 13819 MILWAUKEE, WI 53213

Visit Hal Leonard Online at
www.halleonard.com

2

CONTENTS

All Apologies

Words and Music by Kurt Cobain

recorded by Nirvana

What else should I be? All apologies.
What else should I say? Everyone is gay.
What else should I write? I don't have the right.
What else should I be? All apologies.

Refrain:
In the sun, in the sun I feel as one.
In the sun, in the sun I'm married, buried.

I wish I was like you, easily amused.
Find my nest of salt. Everything is my fault.
I'll take all the blame, aqua sea foam shame.
Sunburn with freezer burn. Choking on the ashes of her enemy.

Refrain

Married, buried. Yeah, yeah, yeah, yeah.

Sing 4 times:
All alone is all we all are.
All alone is all we all are.

All alone is all we all are.
All alone is all we all are.
All alone is all we all…
All alone is all we all are.
All alone is all we all are.

Always Be My Baby

Words and Music by Mariah Carey, Jermaine Dupri and Manuel Seal

recorded by Mariah Carey

We were as one, babe, for a moment in time.
And it seemed everlasting, that you would always be mine.
Now you want to be free, so, I'll let you fly,
'Cause I know in my heart, babe, our love will never die.

Refrain:
You'll always be a part of me. I'm part of you indefinitely.
Boy, don't you know you can't escape me.
Ooh, darling, 'cause you'll always be my baby.
And we'll linger on. Time can't erase a feeling this strong.
No way you're ever gonna shake me.
Ooh, darling, 'cause you'll always be my baby.

I ain't gonna cry, no, and I won't beg you to stay.
If you're determined to leave, boy, I will not stand in your way.
But inevitably you'll be back again,
'Cause you know in your heart, babe, our love will never end.

Refrain

I know that you'll be back, boy,
When your days and your nights get a little bit colder.
I know that you'll be right back, baby.
Baby, believe me, it's only a matter of time, time.

Refrain

All 4 Love

Words and Music by Isaac Hayes, Steve Cropper, Howard Thompson,
   Bryan Kyeth Abrams, Mark Calderon, Sam Watters and Kevin Kraig Thornton

recorded by Color Me Badd

I'm so glad you're my girl, I'll do anything for you.
Call you every night and give you flowers too.
I thank the Lord for you and think about you all the time,
And ask Him every day that you'll forever be mine.
I wanna hold your hand to show you I'll be there.
I like to do the things that let you know I care.

I sing this lullabye 'cause girl, you fill me full.
I look into your eyes, you're so beautiful.
Oh, girl, I think I love ya.
I'm always thinking of ya.
I want you to know I do it all for love.
I love it when we're together.
Girl, I need you forever,
And I want you to know I do it all for love.

I will never leave you, sugar, this I guarantee.
I look into the future, I see you and me.
Knight in shining armor, I will be your fairy tale.
I wanna take care of you, girl, I'll serve you well.
I will be there for ya, to catch you when you fall
I'll hold you in my arms; that's where you belong.

I sing this lullabye 'cause girl, you fill me full.
I look into your eyes, you're so beautiful.
Beautiful…yeah!
Oh, girl, I think I love ya.
I'm always thinking of ya.
I want you to know I do it all for love.
I love it when we're together.
Girl, I need you forever,
And I want you to know I do it all for love.

All, all, all, all, all, all, all, all.
Spoken: Yo! Come here sweetheart.
I want you to know something, alright.
See, every day in my life without you would
Be like a hundred years.

Sung: All, all, all, all, all, all, all, all.
Spoken: The distance between us, an ocean of tears.
See, all the things I do for you are for love. Dig it.
Sung: All for lovin', all for you.
All for lovin' you, you, you, you.

Repeat and Fade:
Oh, girl, I think I love ya.
I'm always thinking of ya.
I want you to know I do it all for love.
I love it when we're together.
Girl, I need you forever,
And I want you to know I do it all for love.

...Baby One More Time

Words and Music by Max Martin

recorded by Britney Spears

Oh, baby, baby. Oh, baby, baby.

Oh, baby, baby, how was I supposed to know
That something wasn't right here?
Oh, baby, baby, I shouldn't have let you go.
And now you're out of sight, yeah.

Refrain:
Show me how you want it to be.
Tell me, baby, 'cause I need to know now.
Oh, because my loneliness is killing me, and I,
I must confess I still believe (still believe)
That when I'm not with you I lose my mind.
Give me a sign. Hit me, baby, one more time.

Oh, baby, baby, the reason I breathe is you.
Boy, you've got me blinded.
Oh, pretty baby, there's nothing that I wouldn't do.
It's not the way I planned it.

Refrain

Oh, baby, baby. Oh, baby, baby.

Oh, baby, baby, how was I supposed to know?
Oh, pretty baby, I shouldn't have let you go.
I must confess that my loneliness is killing me now.
Don't you know I still believe that you will be here
And give me a sign. Hit me, baby, one more time.

My loneliness is killing me, and I,
I must confess I still believe (still believe)
That when I'm not with you I lose my mind.
Give me a sign. Hit me, baby, one more time.

I must confess that my loneliness is killing me now.
Don't you know I still believe that you will be here
And give me a sign. Hit me, baby, one more time.

Back at One

Words and Music by Brian McKnight

recorded by Brian McKnight

It's undeniable that we should be together.
It's unbelievable how I used to say that I'd fall never.
The basis is need to know.
If you don't know just how I feel,
Then let me show you now that I'm for real.
If all things in time, time will reveal. Yeah.

Refrain:
One, you're like a dream come true.
Two, just wanna be with you.
Three, girl, it's plain to see
That you're the only one for me.
And four, repeat steps one through three.
Five, make you fall in love with me.
If ever I believe my work is done,
Then I'll start back at one. Yeah.

It's so incredible, the way things work themselves out.
And all emotional, once you know what it's all about, hey.
And undesirable, for us to be apart.
Never would have made it very far,
'Cause you know you've got the keys to my heart. 'Cause

Refrain

Say farewell to the dark of night; I see the coming of the sun.
I feel like a little child whose life has just begun.
You came and breathed new life into this lonely heart of mine.
You threw out the lifeline, just in the nick of time.

Refrain

Blue

Words and Music by Bill Mack

recorded by LeAnn Rimes

Blue, oh, so lonesome for you.
Why can't you be blue over me?
Blue, oh, so lonesome for you.
Tears fill my eyes till I can't see.

Three o'clock in the morning, here am I,
Sitting here so lonely,
So lonesome I could cry.
Blue, oh, so lonesome for you.
Why can't you be blue for me?

Now that it's over, I realized
Those weak words you whispered
Were nothing but lies.
Blue, oh, so lonesome for you.
Why can't you be blue over me?
Why can't you be blue over me?

Barely Breathing

Words and Music by Duncan Sheik

recorded by Duncan Sheik

Well, I know what you're doing. I see it all too clear.
I only taste the saline when I kiss away your tears.
You really had me going, wishing on a star.
The black holes that surrounded you are heavier by far.
I believed in your confusion, so completely torn.
It must have been that yesterday was the day that I was born.
There's not much to examine, nothing left to hide.
You really can't be serious, you have to ask me why?
I say goodbye.

Refrain:
'Cause I am barely breathing, and I can't find the air.
Don't know who I'm kidding, imagining you care.
And I could stand here waiting, ooh, for another day.
I don't suppose it's worth the price, it's worth the price,
The price that I would pay.

And everyone keeps asking what's it all about.
It used to be so certain. Now I can't figure us out.
What is this attraction? Don't it fill the day,
And nothing left to reason, and only you to blame.
Will it ever change?

Refrain

But I'm thinking it over anyway.
But I'm thinking it over anyway. Oh.
I come to find I may never know.
A changing mind, is it friend or foe?
I rise above, I sink below,
And every time you come and go.
Please don't come and go.

Refrain

But I'm thinking it over anyway.
But I'm thinking it over anyway.
Oh, and I know what you're doing.
I see it all too clear.

Beautiful in My Eyes

Words and Music by Joshua Kadison

recorded by Joshua Kadison

You're my peace of mind
In this crazy world.
You're everything I've tried to find.
Your love is a pearl.
You're my Mona Lisa, you're my rainbow skies,
And my only prayer is that you realize,
You'll always be beautiful in my eyes.

The world will turn
And the seasons will change,
And all the lessons we will learn
Will be beautiful and strange.
We'll have our fill of tears, our share of sighs.
My only prayer is that you realize,
You'll always be beautiful in my eyes.

You will always be beautiful in my eyes.
And the passing years will show
That you will always grow,
Ever more beautiful in my eyes.

When there are lines upon my face,
From a lifetime of smiles.
When the time comes to embrace
For one long last while;
We can laugh about how time really flies.
We won't say goodbye 'cause true love never dies;
You'll always be beautiful in my eyes.

You'll always be beautiful in my eyes.
And the passing years will show
That you will always grow,
Ever more beautiful in my eyes.

The passing years will show
That you will always grow,
More beautiful in my eyes.

Beauty and the Beast

Lyrics by Howard Ashman
Music by Alan Menken

from Walt Disney's *Beauty And The Beast*
recorded by Celine Dion & Peabo Bryson

Tale as old as time,
True as it can be.
Barely even friends,
Then somebody bends
Unexpectedly.

Just a little change.
Small, to say the least.
Both a little scared,
Neither one prepared.
Beauty and the Beast.
Ever just the same.
Ever a surprise.
Ever as before,
Ever just as sure
As the sun will rise.

Tale as old as time.
Tune as old as song.
Bittersweet and strange,
Finding you can change,
Learning you were wrong.

Certain as the sun
Rising in the East.
Tale as old as time,
Song as old as rhyme.
Beauty and the Beast.

Tale as old as time,
Song as old as rhyme
Beauty and the Beast.

Because of You

Words and Music by Arnthor Birgisson, Christian Karlsson, Patrick Tucker and
  Anders Sven Bagge

recorded by 98 Degrees

It's all.

Refrain:
You're my sunshine after the rain.
You're the cure against my fear and my pain
'Cause I'm losin' my mind when you're not around.
It's all, (it's all) it's all because of you.

You're my sunshine, oh yeah.
Baby, I really know by now.
Since we met that day, you showed me the way.
I felt it then you gave me love.
I can't describe how much I feel for you.
I said, "Baby, I should've known by now,
Should've been right there whenever you gave me love."
And if only you were here I'd tell you,
Yes, I'd tell you, oh yeah.

Refrain

Oh yeah, yeah.
Honestly, could it be you and me like it was before,
Neither less or more?
'Cause when I close my eyes at night
I realize that no one else could ever take your place.
I still can feel and it's so unreal
When you're touchin' me, kisses endlessly.
It's just a place in the sun, where our love's begun.
I'll miss you. Yes, I miss you, oh babe.

Refrain

If I knew how to tell you what's on my mind,
Make you understand, then I'd always be there
Right by your side.

Refrain

Been Caught Stealing

Words and Music by Jane's Addiction

recorded by Jane's Addiction

I've been caught stealing once when I was five.
I enjoy stealing. It's just as simple as that.
A, well, it's just a simple fact.
When I want something and I don't want to pay for it.

Yeah, when I walk right through the door,
And I walk right through the door.
Hey, all right.
If I get by it's mine, mine all mine. Hey.

Yeah, my girl, she's one too. She'll go and get her a skirt.
Stick it under her shirt. She grabbed a razor for me.
And she did it just like that.
When she wants something and she don't want to pay for it.

She walk right through the door,
Walk right through the door.
Hey, all right.
If I get by it's mine, mine all mine. Let's go.

A, la, la, da, da, da, da, da,
Da, da, da, da ,da, da, da, da, da.
A, la, la, da, ba, da, da, da,
Da, da, da, da ,da, da, da, da, da. Brr.

Sat around the pile, sat and laughed,
Sat and laughed and waved it into the air.
And we did it just like that
When we want something and we don't want to pay for it.

We walk right through the door,
Walk right through the door.
Hey, all right.
If I get by it's, a, mine, all mine, all mine, all mine,
All mine, all mine, all mine, all mine, all mine.
It's, a, mine.

Bitch

Words and Music by Meredith Brooks and Shelly Peiken

recorded by Meredith Brooks

I hate the world today.
You're so good to me, I know,
But I can't change.
Tried to tell you, but you look at me
Like maybe I'm an angel underneath,
Innocent and sweet.

Yesterday I cried.
You must have been relieved
To see the softer side.
I can understand how you'd be so confused.
I don't envy you.
I'm a little bit of everything all rolled into one.

Refrain:
I'm a bitch. I'm a lover. I'm a child.
I'm a mother. I'm a sinner. I'm a saint.
I do not feel ashamed.
I'm your hell. I'm your dream.
I'm nothing in between.
You know you wouldn't want it any other way.

So, take me as I am.
This may mean you'll have to
Be a stronger man.
Rest assured that when I start to make you nervous
And I'm going to extremes,
Tomorrow I will change and today won't mean a thing.

Refrain

Just when you think you got me figured out,
The season's already changin'.
I think it's cool, you do what you do,
And don't try to save me.

Refrain

I'm a bitch. I'm a tease.
I'm a goddess on my knees.
When you hurt, when you suffer,
I'm your angel undercover.
I've been numb. I'm revived.
Can't say I'm not alive.
You know I wouldn't want it any other way.

Repeat and Fade:
Oo, oo, oo. Oo, oo, oo.

Black Hole Sun

Words and Music by Chris Cornell

recorded by Soundgarden

In my eyes, indisposed,
In disguise as no one knows,
Hide the face, lies the snake,
And the sun in my disgrace.
Boiling heat, summer stretch.
'Neath black, the sky looks dead.
Call me name through the cream,
And I'll hear you scream again.

Black hole sun, won't you come
And wash away the rain?
Black hole sun, won't you come?
Won't you come? Won't you come?

Stuttering, cold and damp.
Steal the warm wind, tired friend.
Times are gone for honest men,
And sometimes far too long for snakes.
In my shoes, a walking sleep,
And my youth I pray to keep.
Heaven send hell away.
No one sings like you anymore.

Black hole sun, won't you come
And wash away the rain?
Black hole sun, won't you come?
Won't you come? Won't you come?
Won't you come? Won't you come?
Won't you come?

Hang my head, drown my fear,
'Til you all just disappear.
Black hole sun, won't you come
And wash away the rain?
Black hole sun, won't you come?
Won't you come? Won't you come?

Black hole sun, won't you come
And wash away the rain?
Black hole sun, won't you come?
Won't you come? Won't you come?
Won't you come? Won't you come?
Won't you come? Won't you come?

Black Velvet

Words and Music by David Tyson and Christopher Ward

recorded by Alannah Myles

Mississippi in the middle of a dry spell.
Jimmie Rodgers on the Victrola up high.
Mama's dancin' with baby on her shoulder.
The sun is settin' like molasses in the sky.
The boy could sing; knew how to move everything.

Refrain:
Always wanting more.
He'd leave you longing for
Black velvet and that little boy smile.
Black velvet with that slow southern style.
A new religion that'll bring you to your knees.
Black velvet, if you please.

Up in Memphis the music's like a heat wave.
"White Lightnin" bound to drive you wild.
Mama's baby is in the heart of every school girl.
"Love Me Tender" leaves 'em cryin' in the aisle.
The way he moved it was a sin so sweet and true.

Refrain

Every word of every song that he sang was for you.
In a flash he was gone it happened soon.
What could you do?

Black velvet and that little boy smile.
Black velvet in that slow southern style.
A new religion that'll bring you to your knees.
Black velvet, if you please.

Black Velvet and that little boy smile.
Black velvet in that slow southern style.
A new religion that'll bring you to your knees.
Black velvet, if you please.
If you please. If you please.
Mm. Mm.

Blaze of Glory

Words and Music by Jon Bon Jovi

recorded by Jon Bon Jovi

I wake up in the morning and I raise my weary head,
I've got an old coat for a pillow and the earth was last night's bed.
I don't know where I'm going, only God knows where I've been.
I'm a devil on the run, a six-gun lover, a candle in the wind, yeah!

When you're brought into this world they say you're born in sin.
Well, at least they gave me something I didn't have to steal or have to
    win.
Well, they tell me that I'm wanted, yeah, I'm a wanted man.
I'm a colt in your stable, I'm what Cain was to Abel.
Mister, catch me if you can.

I'm going down in a blaze of glory.
Take me now but know the truth.
I'm going out in a blaze of glory.
Lord, I never drew first bit I drew first blood,
And I'm no one's son. Call me young gun.

You ask about my conscience and I offer you my soul.
You ask if I'll grow to be a wise man, well, I ask if I'll grow old.
You ask me if I've known love and what it's like to sing songs in the
    rain.
Well, I've seen love come, I've seen it shot down, I've seen it die in
    vain.

Shot down in a blaze of glory.
Take me now but know the truth.
'Cause I'm going down in a blaze of glory.
Lord, I never drew first bit I drew first blood,
I'm the no devil's son. Call me young gun.

Each night I go to bed, I pray the Lord my soul to keep.
No, I ain't looking for forgiveness, but before I'm six feet deep,
Lord, I got to ask a favor and I hope you'll understand.
'Cause I've lived life to the fullest, let this boy die like a man.
Staring down a bullet, let me make my final stand.

Shot down in a blaze of glory.
Take me now but know the truth.
I'm going out in a blaze of glory.
Lord, I never drew first bit I drew first blood,
And I'm the no one's son,
Call me young gun. I'm a young gun.
Young gun, yeah, yeah, yeah, young gun.

Brick

Words and Music by Ben Folds and Darren Jessee

recorded by Ben Folds Five

Six A.M., day after Christmas,
I throw some clothes on in the dark.
The smell of cold, car seat is freezing,
The world is sleeping, I am numb.

Up the stairs to her apartment,
She is balled up on the couch.
Her mom and dad went down to Charlotte,
They're not home to find us out.

And we drive.
Now that I have found someone,
I'm feeling more alone
Than I ever have before.

She's a brick and I'm drowning slowly
Off the coast and I'm headed nowhere.
She's a brick and I'm drowning slowly.

They call her name at seven-thirty.
I pace around the parking lot,
And I walk down to buy her flowers
And sell some gifts that I got.

Can't you see
It's not me you're dying for?
Now she's feeling more alone
Than she ever has before.

She's a brick and I'm drowning slowly
Off the coast and I'm headed nowhere.
She's a brick and I'm drowning slowly.

As weeks went by they showed that she was not fine.
They told me, "Son, it's time to tell the truth,"
And she broke down and I broke down
'Cause I was tired of lying.

Driving back to her apartment,
For the moment we're alone.
Well, she's alone and I'm alone.
Now I know it.

She's a brick and I'm drowning slowly
Off the coast and I'm headed nowhere.
She's a brick and I'm drowning slowly.

Buddy Holly

Words and Music by Rivers Cuomo

recorded by Weezer

What's with these homies dissin' my girl?
Why do they gotta front?
What did we ever do to these guys
That made them so violent?

(Woo hoo) But you know I'm yours,
(Woo hoo) and I know you're mine,
(Woo hoo and that's for all time.)
Ooh wee ooh, I look just like Buddy Holly.
Oh oh, and you're Mary Tyler Moore.
I don't care what they say about us anyway.
I don't care 'bout that.

Don't you ever fear I'm always near?
I know that you need help.
Your tongue is twisted, your eyes are slit.
You need a guardian.

(Woo hoo) And you know I'm yours,
(Woo hoo) and I know you're mine,
(Woo hoo and that's for all time.)
Ooh wee ooh, I look just like Buddy Holly.
Oh oh, and you're Mary Tyler Moore.
I don't care what they say about us anyway.
I don't care 'bout that. I don't care 'bout that.

Bang, bang, knock on the door,
'Nother big bang, you're down on the floor.
Oh no, what do we do?
Don't look now, but I lost my shoe.
I can't run and I can't kick.
What's the matter, babe, are you feelin' sick?
What's a-matter, what's a-matter, what's a-matter you?
What's a-matter, babe, are you feelin' blue?
Oh, oh, oh, oh, oh, oh, oh.
(And that's for all time. That's for all time.)

Ooh wee ooh, I look just like Buddy Holly.
Oh oh, and you're Mary Tyler Moore.
I don't care what they say about us anyway.
I don't care 'bout that. I don't care 'bout that.
I don't care 'bout that. I don't care 'bout that.

Building a Mystery

Words and Music by Sarah McLachlan and Pierre Marchand

recorded by Sarah McLachlan

You come out at night,
That's when the energy comes
And the dark side' light
And the vampires roam.
You strut your rasta wear
And your suicide poem
And a cross from a faith that died before Jesus came.
You're building a mystery.

You live in a church
Where you sleep with voo-doo dolls,
And you won't give up the search.
For the ghost in the halls.
You wear sandals in the snow
And a smile that won't wash away.
Can you look out the window
Without your shadow getting in the way?
You're so beautiful,
With an edge and a charm,
But so careful when I'm in your arms
'Cause:

Refrain:
You're working building a mystery,
Holding on and holding it in.
Yeah, you're working building a mystery
And choosing so carefully.

You woke up screaming aloud
A prayer from your secret god
To feed off fears
And hold back your tears, oh.
You give us a tantrum
And a know-it-all grin,
Just when you need one
When the evening's thin.
You're a beautiful,
A beautiful, fucked up man.
You're setting up your razor wire shrine
'Cause:

Refrain Three Times

You're building a mystery.

Butterfly Kisses

Words and Music by Bob Carlisle and Randy Thomas

recorded by Bob Carlisle

There's two things I know for sure.
She was sent here from heaven and she's daddy's little girl.
As I drop to my knees by her bed at night,
She talks to Jesus, and I close my eyes,
And I thank God for all of the joy in my life.

Oh, but most of all, for butterfly kisses after bedtime prayer,
Stickin' little white flowers all up in her hair.
"Walk beside the pony Daddy, it's my first ride.
I know the cake looks funny, Daddy, but I sure tried."

Oh, with all that I've done wrong, I must have done something right
To deserve a hug every morning and butterfly kisses at night.

Sweet sixteen today,
She's looking like her momma a little more every day.
One part woman, the other part, girl.
To perfume and make-up from ribbons and curls,
Trying her wings out in a great big world.

But I remember butterfly kisses after bedtime prayer,
Stickin' little white flowers all up in her hair.
"You know how much I love you, Daddy, but if you don't mind,
I'm only goin' to kiss you on the cheek this time."

Oh, with all that I've done wrong, I must have done something right
To deserve her love every morning and butterfly kisses at night.

(All the precious time.)
Like the wind, the years go by.
(Precious butterfly, spread your wings and fly.)

She'll change her name today.
She'll make a promise, and I'll give her away.
Standing in the bride room just staring at her,
She asked me what I'm thinking, and I said, "I'm not sure.
I just feel like I'm losing my baby girl."

Then she leaned over, gave me butterfly kisses with her momma there,
Stickin' little white flowers all up in her hair.
"Walk me down the aisle, Daddy, its just about time.
Does my wedding gown look pretty, Daddy? Daddy, don't cry."

Oh, with all that I've done wrong, I must have done something right
To deserve her love every morning and butterfly kisses.

I couldn't ask God for more. Man, this is what love is.
I know I've gotta let her go, but I'll always remember
Every hug in the morning and butterfly kisses.

Can You Feel the Love Tonight

Music by Elton John
Lyrics by Tim Rice

from Walt Disney Pictures' *The Lion King*
recorded by Elton John

There's a calm surrender
To the rush of the day,
When the heat of the rolling world
Can be turned away.
An enchanted moment,
And it sees me through.
It's enough for this restless warrior
Just to be with you.

Refrain:
And can you feel the love tonight?
It is where we are.
It's enough for this wide-eyed wanderer
That we got this far.
And can you feel the love tonight,
How it's laid to rest?
It's enough to make kings and vagabonds
Believe the very best.

There's a time for everyone,
If they only learn,
That the twisting kaleidoscope
Moves us all in turn.
There's a rhyme and reason
To the wild outdoors,
When the heart of this star-crossed voyager
Beats in time with yours.

Refrain

Closer to Free

Words and Music by Sam Llanas and Kurt Neumann

from *Party of Five*
recorded by BoDeans

Everybody wants to live like they want to live
And everybody wants to love like they want to love.
Everybody wants to be closer to free.

Everybody wants respect, just a little bit.
And everybody needs a chance once in a while.
Everybody wants to be closer to free.

Everybody one, everybody two,
Everybody free.

Everybody needs to touch, you know now and then.
And everybody wants a good, good friend.
Everybody wants to be closer to free.

Everybody one, everybody two,
Everybody free.

Everybody wants to live like they want to live
And everybody wants to love like they want to love.
Everybody wants to be closer to free.

Yeah, closer to free, yeah, closer to free,
Closer to free.

Change the World

Words and Music by Wayne Kirkpatrick, Gordon Kennedy and Tommy Sims

recorded by Eric Clapton

If I can reach the stars, pull one down for you,
Shine it on my heart so you could see the truth.
Then this love I have inside is everything it seems,
But for now I find it's only in my dreams
That I can change the world.
I will be the sunlight in your universe.

You would think my love was really something good,
Baby, if I could
Change the world.

If I could be king, even for a day,
I'd take you as my queen, I'd have it no other way.
And our love will rule in this kingdom we have made.
'Til then I'd be a fool wishing for the day
That I could change the world.

I would be the sunlight in your universe.
You would think my love was really something good,
Baby, if I could
Change the world.

Baby, if I could
Change the world.

I could change the world.
I would be the sunlight in your universe.
You would think my love was really something good,
Baby, if I could,
Change the world,
Baby, if I could
Change the world,
Baby if I could
Change the world.

Come to My Window

Words and Music by Melissa Etheridge

recorded by Melissa Etheridge

Refrain:
Come to my window.
Crawl inside, wait by the light of the moon.
Come to my window.
I'll be home soon.

I would dial the numbers
Just to listen to your breath.
And I would stand inside my hell
And hold the hand of death.
You don't know how far I'd go
To ease this precious ache.
And you don't know how much I'd give
Or how much I can take.
Just to reach you.
Just to reach you.
Oh, to reach you, oh.

Refrain

Keeping my eyes open,
I cannot afford to sleep.
Giving away promises
I know that I can't keep.
Nothing fills the blackness
That has seeped into my chest.
I need you in my blood,
I am forsaking all the rest.
Just to reach you.
Just to reach you.
Oh, to reach you, oh.

Refrain

I don't care what they think.
I don't care what they say.
What do they know about this love anyway?

Come, come to my window,
I'll be home, I'll be home, I'll be home.
I'm coming home.

Refrain

I'll be home, I'll be home, I'm comin' home.

Constant Craving

Words and Music by k.d. lang and Ben Mink

recorded by k.d. lang

Even through the darkest phase, be it thick or thin,
Always someone marches brave here beneath my skin.
And constant craving has always been.

Craving.
Ah, ha, constant craving has always been,
Has always been.

Maybe a great magnet pulls all souls toward truth.
Or maybe it is life itself that feeds wisdom to its youth.
Constant craving has always been.

Craving.
Ah, ha, constant craving has always been,
Has always been.

Constant craving has always been.

Craving.
Ah, ha, constant craving has always been
Has always been.

Creep

Words and Music by Albert Hammond, Mike Hazlewood, Thomas Yorke,
  Richard Greenwood, Philip Selway, Colin Greenwood and Edward O'Brian

recorded by Radiohead

When you were here before, couldn't look you in the eye.
You're just like an angel, your skin makes me cry.
You float like a feather, in a beautiful world.
I wish I were special, you're so fuckin' special.

Refrain:
But I'm a creep, I'm a weirdo.
What the hell am I doing here?
I don't belong here.

I don't care if it hurts, I want to have control.
I want a perfect body, I want a perfect soul.
I want you to notice when I'm not around.
You're so fuckin' special, I wish I were special.

Refrain

Oh, oh, oh. She's running out again.
She's running out. She run, run, run, run. Run.

Whatever makes you happy, whatever you want.
You're so fuckin' special, I wish I were special.

Refrain

I don't belong here.

Counting Blue Cars

Words by J.R. Richards
Music by Scot Alexander, George Pendergast, Rodney Browning,
  J.R. Richards and Gregory Kolanek

recorded by Dishwalla

Must have been late afternoon.
I could tell by how far the child's shadow stretched out.
And he walked with a purpose in his sneakers down the street.
He had many questions like children often do.
He said, "Tell me all your thoughts on God.
And tell me, am I very far?"

Must have been late afternoon.
On our way, the sun broke free of the clouds.
We count only blue cars, skip the cracks in the street
And ask many questions like children often do.
We said, "Tell me all your thoughts on God,
'Cause I'd really like to meet her.
And ask her why we're who we are.
Tell me all your thoughts on God,
'Cause I'm on my way to see her.
So tell me, am I very far, am I very far now?"

It's getting cold, picked up the pace.
How our shoes make hard noises in this place.
Our clothes are stained, we pass money, cross our people,
And ask many questions like children often do.
He said, "Tell me all your thoughts on God,
'Cause I'd really like to meet her
And ask her why we're who we are.
Tell me all your thoughts on God,
'Cause I'm on my way to see her.
So tell me am I very far, am I very far now?"

Repeat and Fade:
"Tell me all your thoughts on God."

Cradle of Love

Words and Music by David Werner and Billy Idol

recorded by Billy Idol

Rock the cradle of love.
Rock the cradle of love.
Yes, the cradle of love don't rock easily, Sue,
Well, rock the cradle of love.
I rock the cradle of love.
Yes, the cradle of love don't rock easily, Sue,well, now.

It burned like a motor on fire
When the rebel took a little child bride to tease, yeah.
So go easy, yeah,
'Cause love cuts a million ways.
Shakes the devil when he missbehaves.
I ain't nobody's fool.
Come on, shake it up, whatever I do.

Rock the cradle of love.
Rock the cradle of love.
Yes, the cradle of love don't rock easily, Sue,
Sent from heaven above, that's right,
To rock the cradle of love.
Yes, the cradle of love, don't talk teasingly, Sue, yeah.

Pledge for your Romeo.
"Oh yeah, baby," I hear you moan, it's easy.
You know how to please me, yeah.
'Cause love starts my rollin' train.
You can't stop me. It ain't in vain.
I ain't nobody's fool.
Come on, shake it up, whatever I do.

These are the wages of love.
Rock the cradle.
These are the wages of love.
Rock the cradle.

Well, it burned like a motor on fire
When the rebel took a little child bride to tease, yeah.
You know how to please you, yeah.
Oh, my heart starts a rollin' train.
You can't stop me. It ain't in vain.
I ain't nobody's fool.
Come on, shake it up, whatever I do.

Rock the cradle of love.
Rock the cradle of love.
Sent from heaven above, that's right.
She rocked the cradle of love.
Rock the cradle of love, yeah.
Cradle of love. That's me, mama.
I'll rob the devil of love, alright.
Cradle of love.
(Rock the cradle of love. Cradle of love.)

Criminal

Words and Music by Fiona Apple

recorded by Fiona Apple

I've been a bad, bad girl;
I've been careless with a delicate man.
And it's a sad, sad world
When a girl will break a boy just because she can.

Don't you tell me to deny it; I've done wrong,
And I wanna suffer for my sins.
I've come to you 'cause I need guidance to be true,
And I just don't know where I can begin.

Refrain:
What I need is a good defense,
'Cause I'm feelin' like a criminal.
And I need to be redeemed to the one I've sinned against
Because he's all I ever knew of love.

Heaven, help me for the way I am;
Save me from these evil deeds before I get them done.
I know tomorrow brings the consequence at hand,
But I keep livin' this day like the next will never come.

Oh, help me, but don't tell me to deny it.
I've gotta cleanse myself of all these lies
'Til I'm good enough for him.
I've got a lot to lose and I'm betting high,
So I'm begging you, before it ends,
Just tell me where to begin.

Refrain

Let me know the way before there's hell to pay.
Give me room to lay the law and let me go.
I've got to make a play to make my lover stay,
So what would an angel say, the devil wants to know.

Refrain Twice

Damn, I Wish I Was Your Lover

Words and Music by Sophie B. Hawkins

recorded by Sophie B. Hawkins

That old dog has chained you up all right.
Give you everything you need to
Live inside a twisted cage,
Sleep beside an empty rage.
I had a dream I was your hero.

Damn, I wish I was your lover.
I'd rock you 'til the daylight comes,
Make sure you are smiling and warm.
I am everything. Tonight I'll be your mother.
I'll do things to ease your pain,
Free you from your mind and you won't feel ashamed.
Oh. Open up, coming inside,
Gonna fill you up, gonna make you cry. Uh huh.

This monkey can't stand to see you black and blue.
I'll give you something sweet each time you
Come inside my jungle book.
What is it, just too good?
Don't say you'll stay 'cause then you'll go away.

Damn, I wish I was your lover.
I'd rock you 'til the daylight comes,
Make sure you are smiling and warm.
I am everything. Tonight I'll be your mother.
I'll do things to ease your pain,
Free you from your mind and you won't feel ashamed.
Shucks, for me there is no other. You're the only shoe that fits.
I can't imagine I'll grow out of it.

Damn, I wish I was your lover.
If I was your girl, believe me.
I'd turn on the Rolling Stones.
We could groove along and feel much better.
Let me in. Mm, mm, mm.
I could do it forever and ever and ever and ever.
Give me an hour to kiss you.
Walk through heaven's door I'm sure.
Don't need no doctor to feel much better.
Let me in. Ooh. I wanna live.
Forever and ever and ever and ever.
I sat on the mountainside with peace of mind.
And I laid by the ocean making
Love to her with visions clear,
Walked for days with no one near.
And I return as chained and bound to you.

Damn, I wish I was your lover.
I'd rock you 'til the daylight comes,
Make sure you are smiling and warm.
I am everything. Tonight I'll be your mother.
I'll do things to ease your pain,
Free you from your mind and you won't feel ashamed.
Shucks, for me there is no other. You're the only shoe that fits.
I can't imagine I'll grow out of it.

Damn, I wish I was your lover.
I'm gonna open up. I wanna come inside.
I'm gonna fill you up. I wanna make you cry.

Damn, I wish I was your lover.
I'm on a subway and I'm comin' up town.
Damn, I wish I was your lover.
Standing on a street corner,
Waiting for my life to change.

Damn, I wish I was your lover
And I'm feeling like a school boy,
Too shy and too young. Oh.
Damn, I wish I was your lover.
Tryin' to open up, I wanna come inside,
Gonna fill you up, I'm gonna make you cry.

Damn, I wish I was your lover.
I'm getting on my camel and I'm ridin' up town.
Damn, I wish I was your lover.
Standing on a street corner,
Waiting for my life to change.

Damn, I wish I was your lover
And I'm feeling like a school boy,
Too shy and too young. Oh.
Damn, I wish I was your lover.
Tryin' to open up, I wanna come inside,
Gonna fill you up, I'm gonna make you cry.

Don't Speak

Words and Music by Eric Stefani and Gwen Stefani

recorded by No Doubt

You and me, we used to be together,
Every day together, always.
I really feel that I'm losing my best friend.
I can't believe this could be the end.
It looks as though you're letting go,
And if it's real, well, I don't want to know.

Refrain:
Don't speak, I know just what you're saying,
So please stop explaining.
Don't tell me 'cause it hurts. No, no, no.
Don't speak, I know what you're thinking.
I don't need your reasons.
Don't tell me 'cause it hurts.

Our memories, they can be inviting,
But some are altogether mighty fright'ning.
As we die, both you and I,
With my head in my hands I sit and cry.

Refrain

It's all ending, I gotta stop pretending who we are.
You and me, I can see us dying…are we?

Refrain

Don't Look Back in Anger

Words and Music by Noel Gallagher

recorded by Oasis

Slip inside the eye of your mind,
Don't you know you might find a better place to play.
You said that you'd never been
But all the things that you've seen slowly fade away.

So I start a revolution from my bed.
'Cause you said the brains I had went to my head.
Step outside, summertime's in bloom,
Stand up beside the fireplace, take that look from off your face,
You ain't ever gonna burn my heart out.

So Sally can wait, she knows it's too late
As we're walking on by her soul slides away.
But don't look back in anger, I heard you say.

Take me to the place where you go
Where nobody knows if it's night or day.
Please don't put your life in the hands
Of a rock'n roll band who'll throw it all away.

I'm gonna start a revolution from my head.
'Cause you said the brains I had went to my head.
Step outside, summertime's in bloom,
Stand up beside the fireplace, take that look from off your face,
'Cause you ain't ever gonna burn my heart out.

So Sally can wait, she knows it's too late
As we're walking on by her soul slides away.
But don't look back in anger, I heard you say.

So Sally can wait, she knows it's too late
As we're walking on by her soul slides away.
But don't look back in anger, don't look back in anger,
I heard you say it's not too late.

Don't Turn Around

Words and Music by Diane Warren and Albert Hammond

recorded by Ace of Base

If you wanna leave, I won't beg you to stay.
And if you gotta go darlin', maybe it's better that way.
I'm gonna be strong, I'm gonna do fine,
Don't worry about this heart of mine.
Spoken: Walk out that door. See if I care. Go on and go.
Sung: But—

Refrain:
Don't turn around, 'cause you're gonna see my heart breakin'.
Don't turn around, I don't want you seein' me cry.
Just walk away, it's tearin' me apart that you're leavin'.
I'm letting you go, but I won't let you know.

I won't let you know.

I won't miss arms around me holding me tight.
And if you ever think about me just know that I'll be all right.
I'm gonna be strong, I'm gonna do fine,
Don't worry about this heart of mine.
Spoken: I know I'll survive. I'll make it through.
I'll even learn to live without you.

Refrain

I wish I could scream out loud that I love you.
I wish I could say to you, "Don't go."
Spoken: As he walks away he feels the pain gettin' strong.
People in your life, they don't know what's goin' on.
Too proud to turn around, he's gone.

Refrain

Baby, don't turn around.

Repeat and Fade:
Don't turn around. Just walk away.
Still the thought that you're leavin',
I'm letting you go.

Emotions

Words and Music by Mariah Carey, David Cole and Robert Clivilles

recorded by Mariah Carey

Refrain:
You've got me feeling emotions,
Deeper than I've ever dreamed of.
Whoa, oh.
You've got me feeling emotions,
Higher than the heavens above.

I feel good, I feel nice.
I never felt so satisfied.
I'm in love, I'm alive.
Intoxicated, flying high.
It feels like a dream,
When you touch me tenderly.
I don't know if it's real,
But I like the way I feel inside.

Refrain

In the morning when I rise,
You are the first thing on my mind.
And in the middle of the night
I feel you heartbeat next to mine.
It feels like a dream
When you love me tenderly.
I don't know if you're for real
But I like the way I feel.

Refrain

You know the way to make me lose control.
When you're looking into my eyes
You make me feel so high!

Refrain

You've got me feeling higher.

Every Road Leads Back to You

Words and Music by Diane Warren

recorded by Bette Midler

Old friend, here we are,
After all the years and tears
And all that we've been through.
It feels so good to see you.
Looking back in time,
There've been other friends and other lovers,
But no other one like you.
All my life, no one ever has known me better.

Refrain:
I must have traveled down a thousand roads.
Been so many places, seen so many faces,
Always on my way to something new.
But it doesn't matter
'Cause no matter where I go,
Every road leads back,
Every road just seems to lead me back to you.

Old friend, there were times
I didn't want to see your face
Or hear your name again.
Now those times are far behind me.
It's so good to see your smile,
I'd forgotten how nobody else
Could make me smile the way you do.
All this time, you're the one I still want beside me.

Refrain

I must have traveled down a thousand roads.
Been so many places, seen so many faces,
Always on my way to something new.
But it doesn't matter
'Cause no matter where I go,
Every road leads back,
Every road just seems to lead me back.
Every road leads back;
Every road just seems to lead me back to you.
Every road just seems to lead me back to you.

Exhale (Shoop Shoop)

Words and Music by Babyface

from the Original Soundtrack Album *Waiting to Exhale*
recorded by Whitney Houston

Verse 1:
Everyone falls in love sometimes.
Sometimes it's wrong
And sometimes it's right.
For every win
Someone must fail,
But there comes a point when,
When we exhale, yeah, yeah.

Refrain:
Say, shoop shoop shoop shoo be doo…

Verse 2:
Sometimes you'll laugh,
Sometimes you'll cry.
Life never tells us the whens or whys.
When you've got friends
To wish you well,
You'll find a point when
You will exhale, yeah, yeah.

Refrain

Hearts are often broken
When there are words unspoken.
In your soul there's answers to your prayers.
If you're searching for a place you know,
A familiar face, somewhere to go,
You should look inside your soul,
You're halfway there.

Repeat Verse 2 and Refrain

Fields of Gold

Music and Lyrics by Sting

recorded by Sting

You'll remember me
When the west wind moves
Upon the fields of barley.
You'll forget the sun
In his jealous sky
As we walk in fields of gold.

So she took her love
For to gaze awhile
Upon the fields of barley.
In his arms she fell
As her hair came down
Among the fields of gold.

Will you stay with me,
Will you be my love
Among the fields of barley?
We'll forget the sun
In his jealous sky
As we lie in fields of gold.

See the west wind move
Like a lover so
Upon the fields of barley.
Feel her body rise
When you kiss her mouth
Among the fields of gold.

I never made promises lightly
And there have been some that I've broken,
But I swear in the days still left
We'll walk in fields of gold.
We'll walk in fields of gold.

Many years have passed
Since those summer days
Among the fields of barley.
See the children run
As the sun goes down
Among the fields of gold.

You'll remember me
When the west wind moves
Upon the fields of barley.
You can tell the sun
In his jealous sky
When we walked in fields of gold.
When we walked in fields of gold.

Fly to the Angels

Words and Music by Mark Slaughter and Dana Strum

recorded by Slaughter

Pictures of you, oh, they're still on my mind.
You had the smile that could light up the world.
Now it rains; it seems the sun never shines.
And I'll drive down this lonely, lonely road.
Oo, I got this feelin'. Girl, I've gotta let you go.

Refrain:
'Cause now you've got to fly. (Fly high.)
Fly to the angels.
Heaven awaits your heart and flowers bloom in your name.
Whoa. You've got to fly. (Fly high.)
Fly to the angels.
All the stars in the night shine in your name.

You know it hurts me way deep inside.
When I turn and look and find that you're not there.
I try to convince myself that the pain, the pain, it's still not gone.
And I'll drive down this lonely, lonely road.
Oo, I got this feelin'. Girl, I've gotta let you go.

Refrain

Ooh. Oh, yeah.
Ooh, yeah! Ooh, yeah.
And still I drive down this lonely, lonely road.
Oo, I got this feelin'. Girl, I've gotta let you go.

Refrain

Yeah! Ow! Ooh. Ooh. Ooh, ooh, ooh.
Baby. Ow. Ooh.Ooh. Ooh, ooh, ooh.
Ooh, yeah! Ooh. Ooh. Ooh. Ooh, ooh, ooh.
I'm gonna miss you. Miss you girl.

Gettin' Jiggy wit It

Words and Music by Nile Rodgers, Bernard Edwards, Will Smith,
  Samuel J. Barnes and J. Robinson

Recorded by Will Smith

Bring it…woo…uh, uh, uh, uh.
Ha, ha, ha, ha!
What , what, what, what?
Ha, ha, ha, ha!

On your mark, ready, set, let's go.
Dance floor pro, I know you know.
I go psycho when my new joint hit.
Just can't sit.
Gotta get jiggy wit' it.
Ooh, that's it.
Now honey, honey, come ride.
DKNY all up in my eye.
You gotta Prada bag with a lotta stuff in it,
Give it to your friend, let's spin.
Everybody lookin' at me,
Glancin' at the kid,
Wishin' they was dancin' a jig
Here with this handsome kid.
Cigar-cigar right from Cuba-Cuba.
I just bite it.
It's for the look, I don't light it.
Ill-way to 'Ami on the ance-day oor-flay.
Yo, my cardio is infinite. (Ha, ha!)
Big Willie style's all in it.
Gettin' jiggy wit' it.

Refrain:
Na, na, na…gettin' jiggy wit' it.
Na, na, na…gettin' jiggy wit' it.

What? You wanna ball with the kid?
Watch your step, you might fall tryin' to do what I did.
Mama, uh, mama, uh, mama come closer.
In the middle of the club with the rub-a-dub.
No love for the haters, the haters,
Mad 'cause I got floor seats at the Lakers.
See me on the fifty-yard line with the Raiders.
Met Ali, he told me, I'm the greatest.
I got the fever for the flavor of a crowd pleaser.
DJ play another from the prince of this.
Your highness, only mad chicks ride in my whips.
South to the west to the east to the north,
Bought my hits and watch 'em go off, a-go off.
Ah yes, yes y'all, ya don't stop,
In the winter or the (summertime),
I makes it hot.
Gettin' jiggy wit' 'em.

Refrain

Eight-fifty I.S., if you need a lift.
Who's the kid in the drop?
Who else? Will Smith,
Living that life some consider a myth.
Rock from South Street to one two fifth,
Women used to tease me,
Give it to me now nice and easy,
Since I moved up like George and Weezy.
Dream to the maximum, I be askin' 'em,
"Would you like to bounce with the brother that's platinum?"
Never see Will attackin' 'em,
Rather play ball with Shaq and 'em,
Flatten 'em.

Psyche.
Kiddin'.
You thought I took a spill, but I didn't.
Trust the lady of my life, she's hittin',
Hit her with a drop top with the ribbon,
Crib for my mom on the outskirts of Philly.
You tryin' to flex on me?
Don't be silly.
Gettin' jiggy wit' it.

Refrain Three Times

The Freshmen

Words and Music by Brian Vander Ark

recorded by The Verve Pipe

When I was young, I knew everything.
She, a punk who rarely ever took advice.
Now I'm guilt stricken, sobbing with my head on the floor.
Stop a baby's breath and a shoeful of rice, now.

Refrain:
I can't be responsible,
'Cause she was touching her face.
I won't be held responsible.
She fell in love in the first place.
For the life of me, I cannot remember
What made us think that we were wise
And we'd never compromise.
For the life of me, I cannot believe
We'd ever die for these sins.
We were merely freshmen.

My best friend took a week's vacation to forget her.
His girl took a week's worth of Valium and slept.
And now he's guilt stricken, sobbing with his head on the floor.
Thinks about her now and how he never really wept. He says,

Refrain

Hey, yeah, yeah, yeah, yeah. Hey, yeah.
Hey, yeah, yeah, yeah, yeah.

We tried to wash our hands of all of this.
We never talk of a lack in relationships
And how we're guilt stricken, sobbing with out heads on the floor.
We fell through the ice when we tried not to slip. We'd say

Refrain

For the life of me, I cannot remember
What made us think that we were wise
And we'd never compromise.
For the life of me, I cannot believe
We'd ever die for these sins.
We were merely freshmen.We were merely freshmen.
We were only freshmen.

From a Distance

Words and Music by Julie Gold

recorded by Bette Midler

From a distance the world looks blue and green,
And the snow-capped mountains white.
From a distance the ocean meets the stream
And the eagle takes to flight.

From a distance there is harmony,
And it echoes through the land.
It's the voice of hope, it's the voice of peace
It's the voice of every man.

Refrain:
God is watching us,
God is watching us,
God is watching us
From a distance.

From a distance we all have enough,
And no one is in need.
There are no guns, no bombs, no diseases,
No hungry mouths to feed.

From a distance we are instruments,
Marching in a common band.
Playing songs of hope, playing songs of peace,
They're the songs of every man.

Refrain

From a distance you look like my friend,
Even though we are at war.
From a distance I can't comprehend
What all this war is for.

From a distance there is harmony,
And it echoes through the land.
It's the voice of hopes, it's the love of loves,
It's the heart of every man.

It's the hope of hopes,
It's the love of loves,
It's the song of every man.

Galileo

Words and Music by Emily Saliers

recorded by Indigo Girls

Galileo's head was on the block,
The crime was looking up the truth.
And as the bomb-shells of my daily fears explode,
I try to trace them to my youth.

And then you had to bring up reincarnation
Over a couple of beers the other night.
And now, I'm serving time for mistakes
Made by another in another lifetime.

Refrain:
How long till my soul gets it right?
Can any human being ever reach that kind of light?
I call on the resting soul of Galileo,
King of night vision, king of insight.

And then I think about my fear of motion
For which I never could explain.
Some other fool across the ocean,
Years ago must have crashed his little airplane.

Refrain

I'm not making a joke.
You know me,
I take everything so seriously.
If we wait for the time till all souls get it right,
Then at least I know there'll be no
Nuclear annihilation in my lifetime.
I'm still not right.

I offer thanks to those before me.
That's all I've got to say.
'Cause maybe you squandered
Big bucks in your lifetime.
Now, I have to pay.
But then again it feels like some sort of inspiration
To let the next life off the hook.
Or she'll say,
"Look what I had to overcome in my last life.
I think I'll write a book."

How long till my soul gets it right?
Can any human being ever reach the highest light?
Except for the resting soul of Galileo,
King of night vision, king of insight.

How long?
How long?
How long?

Genie in a Bottle

Words and Music by Steve Kipner, David Frank and Pam Sheyne

recorded by Christina Aguilera

I feel like I've been locked up tight
For a century of lonely nights
Waiting for someone to release me.
You're lickin' your lips
And blowin' kisses my way.
But that don't mean
I'm gonna give it away,
Baby, baby, baby.

Refrain:
Oh.
Spoken: My body's saying let's go. Oh.
Spoken: But my heart is saying no, no.
Sung: If you wanna be with me,
Baby, there's a price to pay.
I'm a genie in a bottle;
You gotta rub me the right way.
If you wanna be with me,
I can make your wish come true.

You gotta make a big impression.
Gotta like what you do.
I'm a genie in a bottle, baby.
You gotta rub me the right way, honey.
I'm a genie in a bottle, baby.
Come, come, come on and let me out.

Music's playing and the light's down low.
Just one more dance and then we're good to go,
Waiting for someone who needs me.
Hormones racing at the speed of light.
But that don't mean it's gotta be tonight,
Baby, baby, baby.

Refrain

Just come and set me free, baby,
And I'll be with you.
I'm a genie in a bottle, baby.
You gotta rub me the right way, honey.
I'm a genie in a bottle, baby.
Come, come, come on and let me out.
I'm a genie in a bottle, baby.
You gotta rub me the right way, honey.
I'm a genie in a bottle, baby.
come, come, come on and let me out.

Refrain

You gotta make a big impression.
Gotta like what you do.

Refrain

Just come and let me free, baby,
And I'll be with you.
I'm a genie in a bottle, baby.
Come, come, come on and let me out.

Give Me One Reason

Words and Music by Tracy Chapman

recorded by Tracy Chapman

Refrain:
Give me one reason to stay here,
And I'll turn right back around.
Give me one reason to stay here,
And I'll turn right back around.
Said I don't want to leave you lonely;
You got to make me change my mind.

Baby, I got your number.
Oh, and I know that you got mine.
But you know that I called you.
I called too many times.
You can call me, baby.
You can call me anytime.
But you got to call me.

Refrain

I don't want no one to squeeze me.
They might take away my life.
I don't want no one to squeeze me.
They might take away my life.
I just want someone to hold me,
Oh, and rock me through the night.

This youthful heart can love you,
Yes, and give you what you need.
I said this youthful heart can love you,
Oh, and give you what you need.
But I'm too old to go chasing you around,
Wasting my precious energy.

Refrain

Baby, give me just one reason.
Oh, give me just one reason why.
Baby, just give me one reason.
Oh, give me just one reason why I should stay.
Said I told you that I loved you,
And there ain't no more to say.

Have You Ever Really Loved a Woman?

Words and Music by Bryan Adams, Michael Kamen and Robert John Lange

from the Motion Picture *Don Juan DeMarco*
recorded by Bryan Adams

To really love a woman
To understand her, you gotta know her deep inside;
Hear every thought, see every dream,
'N' give her wings when she wants to fly.
Then when you find yourself lyin' helpless in her arms,
Ya know ya really love a woman.

Refrain:
When you love a woman you tell her that she's really wanted.
When you love a woman you tell her that she's the one.
'Cause she needs somebody to tell her
That it's gonna last forever.
So tell me,
Have you ever really, really, really ever loved a woman?

To really love a woman,
Let her hold you 'til ya know how she needs to be touched.
You've gotta breathe her, really taste her,
'Til you can feel her in your blood.
'N' when you can see you unborn children in her eyes,
Ya know ya really love a woman.

Refrain

You got to give her some faith, hold her tight.
A little tenderness, gotta treat her right.
She will be there for you, takin' good care of you.
Ya gotta love your woman...

I Don't Have the Heart

Words and Music by Allan Rich and Jud Friedman

recorded by James Ingram

Your face is beaming.
You say it's 'cause you're dreaming
Of how good it's going to be.
You say you've been around,
And now you've finally found
Everything you've wanted and need in me.

Refrain:
I don't have the heart to hurt you.
It's the last thing I wanna do.
But I don't have the heart to love you,
Not the way you want me to.

Inside I'm dying
To see you crying.
How can I make you understand?
I care about you,
So much about you, baby.
I'm tryin' to say this as gently as I can, 'cause

Refrain

You're so trusting and open,
Hoping that love will start.
But I don't have the heart.
Oh, no, I don't have the heart.

Refrain

I don't have the heart.
Baby, I don't have the heart.
I don't have the heart.

The Heart of the Matter

Words and Music by John David Souther, Don Henley and Mike Campbell

recorded by Don Henley

I got the call today, I didn't want to hear,
But I knew that it would come.
An old, true friend of ours was talkin' on the phone,
She said you found someone.
And I thought of all the bad luck and the struggles we went through
And how I lost me and you lost you.
What are those voices outside love's open door
Makes us throw off our contentment and beg for something more?
I'm learning to live without you now,
But I miss you sometimes.
The more I know, the less I understand.
All the things I thought I knew, I'm learning again.

I've been trying to get down to the heart of the matter,
But my will gets weak and my thoughts seem to scatter.
But I think it's about forgiveness, forgiveness.
Even if, even if you don't love me anymore.

Ah, these times are so uncertain,
There's a yearning undefined...people filled with rage.
We all need a little tenderness.
How can love survive in such a graceless age?

The trust and self-assurance that led to happiness,
They're the very things we kill, I guess.
Pride and competition cannot fill these empty arms,
And the work I put between us doesn't keep me warm.

I'm learning to live without you now,
But I miss you, baby.
The more I know, the less I understand.
All the things I thought I'd figured out, I have to learn again.

I've been trying to get down to the heart of the matter,
But everything changes, and my friends seem to scatter.
But I think it's about forgiveness, forgiveness.
Even if, even if you don't love me anymore.

There are people in your life who've come and gone,
They let you down, you know they've hurt your pride.
You better put it all behind you 'cause life goes on.
You keep carryin' that anger, it'll eat you up inside, baby.

I've been trying to get down to the heart of the matter,
But my will gets weak and my thoughts seem to scatter.
But I think it's about forgiveness, forgiveness.
Even if, even if you don't love me.

I've been tryin' to get down to the heart of the matter,
Because the flesh will get weak and the ashes will scatter.
So I'm thinkin' about forgiveness, forgiveness.
Even if, even if you don't love me.

Here and Now

Words and Music by Terry Steele and David Elliot

recorded by Luther Vandross

One look in your eyes,
And there I see
Just what you mean to me.
Here in my heart I believe
Your love is all I ever need.
Holding you close through the night,
I need you. Yeah.

I look in your eyes and there I see
What happiness really means.
The love that we share makes life so sweet.
Together we'll always be.
This pledge of love feels so right,
And ooh, I need you. Yeah.

Refrain:
Here and now,
I promise to love faithfully.
You're all I need.
Here and now,
I vow to be one with thee.
Your love is all I need.

Stay.

When I look in your eyes
And there I see
All that a love should really be.
And I need you more and more each day.
Nothing can take your love away.
More than I dare to dream.
I need you.

Refrain

Starting here.
Ooh, and I'm starting now.
I believe (I believe)
Starting here.
I'm starting right here.
Starting now.
Right now because I believe in your love,
So I'm glad to take the vow.

Refrain

Hero

Words and Music by Mariah Carey and Walter Afanasieff

recorded by Mariah Carey

There's a hero
If you look inside your heart.
You don't have to be afraid
Of what you are.
There's an answer
If you reach into your soul
And the sorrow that you know
Will melt away.

Refrain:
And then a hero comes along
With the strength to carry on
And you cast your fears aside
And you know you can survive.
So, when you feel like hope is gone
Look inside you and be strong
And you'll finally see the truth
That a hero lies in you.

It's a long road
When you face the world alone.
No one reaches out a hand
For you to hold.
You can find love
If you search within yourself
And the emptiness you felt
Will disappear.

Refrain

Lord knows
Dreams are hard to follow,
Don't let anyone tear them away.
Hold on,
There will be tomorrow.
In time you'll find the way.

Refrain

Hey Leonardo
(She Likes Me For Me)

Words and Music by Eliot Sloan, Jeff Pence and Emosia

recorded by Blessid Union of Souls

She don't care about my car
And she don't care about my money.
And that's really good
'Cause I don't got a lot to spend.
But if I did, it wouldn't mean nothin'.

She likes me for me,
Not because I look like Tyson Beckford
With the charm of Robert Redford
Oozing out my ears.
But what she sees are my faults and indecisions,
My insecure conditions
And the tears upon the pillow that I shed.
She don't care about my big screen
Or my collection of DVDs.
Things like that just never mattered much to her.
Plus, she don't watch too much TV.

And she don't care that I can fly her
To places she ain't never been.
But if she really wants to go,
I think deep down she knows that
All she has to say is when.

She likes me for me,
Not because I hang with Leonardo
Or that guy who played in *Fargo*.
I think his name is Steve.
She's the one for me and I just can't live without her.

My arms belong around her
And I'm so glad I found her once again.
And I'm so glad I found her once again.
Yeah, I'm so glad I found her once again.

Gazing at the ceiling
As we entertain our feelings in the dark.
The things that we're afraid of
Are gonna show us what we're made of in the end.

She likes me for me
Not because I sing like Pavarotti
Or because I'm such a hottie.
I like her for her,
Not because she's phat like Cindy Crawford.
She has got so much to offer.
Why does she waste all her time with me?
There must be something there that I don't see.
I don't see.

She likes me for me,
Not because I'm tough like Dirty Harry,
Make her laugh just like Jim Carrey
Unlike the Cable Guy.
But what she sees is that I can't live without her.

My arms belong around her
And I'm so glad I found her once again.
Found her once again. Once again.
Yeah, I'm so glad I found her once again.

Hold On

Words and Music by Carnie Wilson, Chynna Phillips and Glen Ballard

recorded by Wilson Phillips

I know there's pain.
Why do you lock yourself up in these chains?
No one can change your life except for you.
Don't ever let anyone step all over you.
Just open your heart and your mind, mm.
Is it really fair to feel this way inside? Whoa,

Someday somebody's gonna make you wanna turn around and say
    goodbye.
Until then, baby, are you gonna let him hold you down and make you
    cry?
Don't you know things could change?
Things'll go your way if you hold on for one more day.
Can you hold on for one more day?
Things'll go your way. Hold on for one more day.

You could sustain.
Mm, or are you comfortable with the pain?
You've got no one to blame for your unhappiness.
No, baby, you got yourself into your own mess, ooh,
Lettin' your worries pass you by, baby.
Don't you think it's worth your time to change you mind? No, no,

Someday somebody's gonna make you wanna turn around and say
  goodbye.
Until then, baby, are you gonna let him hold you down and make you
  cry?
Don't you know things could change?
Things'll go your way if you hold on for one more day.
Can you hold on for one more day?
Things'll go your way. Hold on for one more day.

I know that there is pain,
But ya hold on for one more day,
And ya break free from the chains.
Yeah, I know there is pain,
But ya hold on for one more day,
And ya break free, break from the chains.

Someday somebody's gonna make you wanna turn around and say
  goodbye.
Until then, baby, are you gonna let him hold you down and make you
  cry?
Don't you know things could change?
Things'll go your way if you hold on for one more day, yeah.
Hold on, don't you know, things could change?
Things could go your way if you hold on for one more day,
If you hold on. Can you hold on?

How Am I Supposed to Live Without You

Words and Music by Michael Bolton and Doug James

recorded by Michael Bolton

I could hardly believe it
When I heard the news today.
I had to come and get it straight from you.
They said you were leavin'
Someone's swept your heart away.
From the look upon your face
I see it's true.
So tell me all about it
Tell me 'bout the plans you makin',
Oh, tell me one thing more
Before I go.

Refrain:
Tell me how am I supposed to live without you,
Now that I've been lovin' you so long?
How am I supposed to live without you?
And how am I supposed to carry on,
When all that I've been living for is gone?

I'm too proud for crying,
Didn't come here to break down.
It's just a dream of mine is comin' to an end.
And how can I blame you
When I built my world around
The hope that one day we'd be
So much more than friends?
I don't want to know the price
I'm gonna pay for dreamin'
Oh, even now,
It's more than I can take.

Refrain

Now I don't wanna face the price
I'm gonna pay for dreamin'
Oh, now that your dream has come true.

How Bizarre

Words and Music by Alan Jansson and Paul Fuemana

recorded by OMC

Spoken:
Brother Pele's in the back, sweet Zina's in the front,
Cruising down the freeway in the hot, hot sun.
TV news and cameras, there's choppers in the sky.
Marines, police, reporters ask, "Where, for and why."
Suddenly, red blue lights flash us from behind.
Loud voice booming, "Please step out onto the line."
Pele preach words of comfort. Zina just hides her eyes.
Policeman taps his shades, "Is that a Chevy '69?"
How bizarre. How bizarre, how bizarre.
Destination unknown as we pull in for some gas.
A freshly pasted poster reveals a smile for the pack.
Elephants and acrobats, lions, snakes, monkey.
Pele speaks righteous. Sister Zina says, "Funky."
How bizarre. How bizarre, how bizarre.

Sung:
Ooh, baby, (ooh, baby) it's making me crazy.
(It's making me crazy.)
Every time I look around, (look around,)
Every time I look around, (every time I look around,)
Every time I look around, it's in my face.

Spoken:
Ringmaster steps out, says, "The elephants left town."
People jump and jive, found the clowns have stuck around.
Pele yells, "We're outta here." Zina says, "Right on."
Making moves and starting grooves before they knew we're gone.
Jumped into the Chevy, headed for big lights.
Wanna know the rest? Hey, buy the rights.
How bizarre. How bizarre, how bizarre.

Refrain

It's in my face.

I Believe in You and Me

Words and Music by David Wolfert and Sandy Linzer

from the Touchstone Motion Picture *The Preacher's Wife*
recorded by Whitney Houston

I believe in you and me.
I believe that we will be
In love eternally.
Well, as far as I can see,
You will always be
The one for me,
Oh, yes, you will.

And I believe in dreams again.
I believe that love will never end.
And like the river finds the sea,
I was lost, now I'm free
'Cause I believe in you and me.

I will never leave your side.
I will never hurt your pride.
When all the chips are down,
Babe, then I will always be around.
Just to be right where you are, my love.

You know I love you, boy.
I'll never leave you out.
I will always let you in, boy,
Oh, baby, to places no one's ever been.
Deep inside, can't you see
That I believe in you and me.

Maybe I'm a fool to feel the way I do.
I would play the fool forever
Just to be with you forever.
I believe in miracles
And love's a miracle,
And yes, baby, you're my dream come true.

I, I was lost, now I'm free,
Oh baby,
'Cause
I believe, I do believe in you and me.
See, I'm lost, now I'm free
'Cause I believe in you and me.

I Can't Dance

Words and Music by Mike Rutherford, Phil Collins and Tony Banks

recorded by Genesis

Hot sun beating down
Burning my feet just walking around.
Hot sun making me sweat.
'Gator's getting close, hasn't got me yet.

I can't dance. I can't talk.
Only thing about me is the way I walk.
I can't dance, I can't sing.
I'm just standing here selling everything.

Blue jeans sitting on the beach,
Her dog's talking to me but she's out of reach.
Oo, she's got a body under that shirt
But all she wants to do is rub my face in the dirt.

'Cause I can't dance. I can't talk.
Only thing about me is the way I walk.
I can't dance, I can't sing.
I'm just standing here selling.
Oh, and checking everything is in place.
You never know who's a looking on.

Young punk spilling beer on my shoes,
Fat guy's talking to me tryin' to steal my blues.
Thick smoke, see her smiling through.
I never thought so much could happen just shooting pool.

But I can't dance. I can't talk.
Only thing about me is the way I walk.
I can't dance, I can't sing.
I'm just standing here selling everything.

'Cause I can't dance. I can't talk.
Only thing about me is the way I walk.
I can't dance, I can't sing.
I'm just standing here selling.
Oh, and checking everything is in place.
You never know who's a looking on.
A perfect body with a perfect face, mm, mm.

No, I can't dance. I can't talk.
Only thing about me is the way I walk.
No, I can't dance, I can't sing.
I'm just standing here selling everything.
And but I can't walk. And no I can't dance.
No, no, no, I can't dance. No, I said I can't sing.

I Do (Cherish You)

Words and Music by Robert Stegall and Dan Hill

recorded by 98 Degrees

I do, I do. I do, I do. Mm.

All I am, all I'll be, everything in this world,
All that I'll ever need is in your eyes shining at me.
When you smile I can feel all my passion unfolding.
Your hand brushes mine and a thousand sensations
Seduce me 'cause I, I do cherish you.

For the rest of my life you don't have to think twice.
I will love you still, from the depths of my soul.
It's beyond my control. I've waited so long to say this to you.
If you're asking do I love you this much, I do.
Oh, baby. Oh.

In my world before you, I lived outside my emotions.
Didn't know where I was going till that day I found you.
How you opened my life to a new paradise.
In a world torn by change, still with all my heart
Till my dying day, I do, cherish you.

I Don't Want to Wait

Words and Music by Paula Cole

featured in "Dawson's Creek"
recorded by Paula Cole

Refrain 1:
So open up your morning light
And say a little prayer for I.
You know that if we are to stay alive,
Then see the peace in every eye.

She had two babies, one was six months,
One was three, in the war of forty-four.
Every telephone ring, every heartbeat stinging
When she thought it was God calling her.
Oh, would her son grow to know his father?

Refrain 2:
I don't want to wait
For our lives to be over.
I want to know right now,
What will it be?
I don't want to wait
For our lives to be over.
Will it be yes,
Or will it be sorry?

For the rest of my life you don't have to think twice.
I will love you still, from the depths of my soul.
It's beyond my control. I've waited so long to say this to you.
If you're asking do I love you this much, yes, I do.
I really love you. I do. I really love you.

If you're asking do I love you this much, baby,
I do cherish you. I'll cherish you, my baby.
This much I know is true.
From the depths of my soul, it's beyond my control.
I've waited so long to say this to you.
If you're asking do I love you this much, baby, I do.
Ah. I do.

(Everything I Do) I Do It for You

Words and Music by Bryan Adams, Robert John Lange and Michael Kamen

from the Motion Picture *Robin Hood: Prince of Thieves*
recorded by Bryan Adams

Look into my eyes,
You will see what you mean to me.
Search your heart, search your soul,
And when you find me there,
You will search no more.
Don't tell me it's not worth trying for.
You can't tell me it's not worth dying for.
You know it's true,
Everything I do,
I do it for you.

Look into my heart,
You will find there's nothing there to hide.
So, take me as I am, take my life,
I would give it all, I would sacrifice.
Don't tell me it's not worth fighting for.
I can't help it, there's nothing I want more.
You know it's true,
Everything I do,
I do it for you.

There's no love like your love,
And no other could give more love.
There's nowhere, unless you're there,
All the time, all the way, yeah.

Oh, you can't tell me it's not worth trying for.
I can't help it, there's nothing I want more.
Yeah, I would fight for you,
I'd lie for you, walk the wire for you,
Yeah, I'd die for you.
You know it's true,
Everything I do,
Oh, oh, I do it for you.

He showed up all wet on the rainy front step
Wearing shrapnel in his skin.
And the war he saw lives inside him still.
It's so hard to be gentle and warm.
The years pass by and now he has granddaughters.

Refrain 2

Oh, so you look at me from across the room.
You're wearing your anguish again.
Believe me, I know the feeling;
It sucks you into the jaws of anger.

Oh, so breathe a little more deeply, my love.
All we have is this very moment,
And I don't want to do what his father,
And his father and his father did.
I want to be here right now.

Refrain 1

Refrain 2

Repeat Refrain 1

I Finally Found Someone

Words and Music by Barbra Streisand, Marvin Hamlisch,
  Robert Lange and Bryan Adams

from *The Mirror Has Two Faces*
recorded by Barbra Streisand & Bryan Adams

He:
I finally found someone
Who knocks me off my feet.
I finally found someone
Who makes me feel complete.

She:
It started over coffee.
We started out as friends.
It's funny how from simple things
The best things begin.

He:
This time it's different.
It's all because of you.
It's better than it's ever been
'Cause we can talk it through.

She:
My favorite line
Was, "Can I call you sometime?"
It's all you had to say
To take my breath away.

Both:
This is it,
Oh, I finally found someone,
Someone to share my life.
I finally found the one
To be with every night.

She: 'Cause whatever I do,
He: It's just got to be you.

Both:
My life has just begun.
I finally found someone.

He: Did I keep you waiting?
She: I didn't mind.
He: I apologize.
She: Baby, that's fine.
He: I would wait forever
Both: Just to know you were mine.
He: You know, I love your hair
She: Are you sure it looks right?
He: I love what you wear.
She: Isn't it too tight?
He: You're exceptional.
Both: I can't wait for the rest of my life.

Both:
This is it.
Oh, I finally found someone,
Someone to share my life.
I finally found someone
To be with every night.

She: 'Cause whatever I do,
He: It's just got to be you.

Both:
My life has just begun.
I finally found someone.

She: And whatever I do,
He: It's just got to be you.
She: My life has just begun.
Both: I finally found someone.

I Wanna Love You Forever

Words and Music by Sam Watters and Louis Biancaniello

recorded by Jessica Simpson

You set my soul at ease, chased darkness out of view,
Left your desperate spell on me.
Say you feel it too, I know you do.
I've got so much more to give.
This can't die, I yearn to live.
Pour yourself all over me
And I'll cherish every drop here on my knees.

Refrain:
I wanna love you forever and this is all I'm asking of you.
Ten thousand lifetimes together, is that so much for you to do?
'Cause from the moment that I saw your face
And felt the fire of your sweet embrace,
I swear I knew, I'm gonna love you forever.

My mind fails to understand what my heart tells me to do.
And I'd give up all I have just to be with you and that would do.
I've always been taught to win and I never thought I'd fall,
Be at the mercy of a man. I've never been.
Now, I only want to be right where you are.

Refrain

In my life I've learned that heaven never waits, no.
Let's take this now before it's gone like yesterday, no.
'Cause when I'm with you there's nowhere else
That I would ever wanna be, no.
I'm breathin' for the next second.
I can feel you lovin' me. I'm gonna love,

Refrain

I Need to Know

Words and Music by Cory Rooney and Marc Anthony

recorded by Marc Anthony

They say around the way you've asked for me.
There's even talk about you wanting me.
I must admit that's what I want to hear,
But that's just talk until you take me there.

Refrain:
Oh, if it's true don't leave me all alone out here
Wondering if you're ever gonna take me there.
Tell me what you're feeling 'cause I need to know.
Girl, you've gotta let me know which way to go
'Cause I need to know. I need to know.
Tell me baby, girl, 'cause I need to know.
I need to know. I need to know.
Tell me, baby girl, 'cause I need to know.

My every thought is of this being true.
It's getting harder not to think of you.
Girl, I'm exactly where I wanna be.
The only thing's I need you here with me.

Refrain

'Cause I need to know. I need to know.
Tell me baby, girl, 'cause I need to know.
I need to know. I need to know.
Tell me, baby girl, 'cause I need to know.

If it's true don't leave me all alone out here
Wondring if you're ever gonna take me there.
Tell me what you're feeling 'cause I need to know.
Girl, you've gotta let me know which way to go
'Cause I need to know. I need to know.
Tell me baby girl, 'cause I need to know.

I Touch Myself

Words and Music by Billy Steinberg, Tom Kelly, Christine Amphlett and
  Mark McEntee

recorded by Divinyls

I love myself, I want you to love me.
When I feel down, I want you above me.
I search myself, I want you to find me.
I forget myself, I want you to remind me.

I don't want anybody else.
When I think about you, I touch myself.
Oh, I don't want anybody else,
Oh no, oh no, oh no.

You're the one who makes me come runnin'.
You're the sun who makes me shine.
When you're around I'm always laughin'.
I wanna make you mine.

I close my eyes and see you before me.
Think I would die if you were to ignore me.
A fool could see how much I adore you.
I'd get down on my knees, I'd do anything for you.

I don't want anybody else.
When I think about you, I touch myself.
Oh, I don't want anybody else,
Oh no, oh no, oh no, yeah.

I love myself, I want you to love me.
When I feel down, I want you above me.
I search myself, I want you to find me.
I forget myself, I want you to remind me.

I don't want anybody else.
When I think about you, I touch myself.
Oh, I don't want anybody else,
Oh no, oh no, oh no.

Spoken: I want you. I don't want anybody else.
And when I think about you, I touch myself.
Ooh. Ooh. Ooh, ooh. Ah.

Sung, Repeat and Fade:
I don't want anybody else.
When I think about you, I touch myself. Oh,

I Want It That Way

Words and Music by Martin Sandberg and Andreas Carlsson

recorded by Backstreet Boys

You are my fire, the one desire.
Believe when I say I want it that way.
But we are two worlds apart.
Can't reach to your heart
When you say that I want it that way.

Refrain:
Tell me why. Ain't nothin' but a heartache.
Tell me why. Ain't nothin' but a mistake.
Tell me why. I never wanna hear you say
I want it that way.

Am I your fire, your one desire?
Yes, I know it's too late,
But I want it that way.

Refrain

Now I can see that we've fallen apart
From the way that it used to be, yeah.
No matter the distance, I want you to know
That deep down inside of me
You are my fire, the one desire.
You are, you are, you are, you are.

Don't wanna hear you say
Ain't nothin' but a heartache.
Ain't nothin' but a mistake.
I never wanna hear you say
I want it that way.

Refrain Twice

I Will Remember You

Words and Music by Sarah McLachlan, Seamus Egan and Dave Merenda

Theme from *The Brothers McMullen*
recorded by Sarah McLachlan

Refrain:
I will remember you.
Will you remember me?
Don't let your life pass you by.
Weep not for the memories.

Remember the good times that we had.
We let them slip away from us when things got bad.
Clearly I first saw you smilin' in the sun.
Wanna feel your warmth upon me. I wanna be the one.

Refrain

I'm so tired but I can't sleep.
Standin' on the edge of something much too deep.
It's funny how I feel so much but I cannot say a word.
We are screaming inside or we can't be heard.

Refrain

I'm so afraid to love you, more afraid to lose,
Clinging to a past that doesn't let me choose.
Well once there was a darkness, a deep and endless night.
You gave me everything you had, oh, you gave me light.

Refrain Twice

Weep not for the memories.

I Will Buy You a New Life

Words by Art Alexakis
Music by Art Alexakis and Everclear

recorded by Everclear

Here is the money that I owe you,
Yes, so you can pay the bills.
I will give you more when I get paid again.
I hate those people who love to tell you,
"Money is the root of all that kills."
They have never been poor.
They have never had the joy of a welfare Christmas.
Yeah. Oh, I know we will never look back. Yeah.

You say you wake up crying,
Yes, and you don't know why.
You get up and you go lay down inside my baby's room.
Yeah, I guess I'm doing okay.
I moved in with the strangest guy.
Can you believe he actually thinks that I am really alive?

I will buy you a garden where your flowers can bloom.
I will buy you a new car, perfect, shiny and new.
I will buy you that big house way up in the West Hills.
I will buy you a new life, yes I will.

Yes, I know all about that other guy,
The handsome man with athletic thighs.
I know about all the times before
With that obsessive little rich boy.
They may make you think you're happy,
Yeah, maybe for a minute or two.
But they can't make you laugh,
No, they can't make you feel the way that I do.

I will buy you a garden where your flowers can bloom.
I will buy you a new car, perfect, shiny and new.
I will buy you that big house way up in the West Hills.
I will buy you a new life. Yeah, I will buy you a new life.
Oh, oh, oh, oh, yeah.

Ooh, I know we can never look back. Yeah. No.
Will you please let me stay the night?
Will you please let me stay the night?
No one will ever know. Yeah, yeah.

Sing twice:
I will buy you a garden where your flowers can bloom.
I will buy you a new car, perfect, shiny and new.
I will buy you that big house way up in the West Hills.
I will buy you a new life, oh yeah.

Repeat and Fade:
I will buy you a new life.

I'd Do Anything for Love (But I Won't Do That)

Words and Music by Jim Steinman

recorded by Meat Loaf

And I would do anything for love.
I'd run right into hell and back.
I would do anything for love.
I'll never lie to you and that's a fact.
But I'll never forget the way you feel right now
Oh, no, no way.
And I would do anything for love,
But I won't do that.
No I won't do that.

Some days it don't come easy,
Some days it don't come hard.
Some days it don't come at all
And these are the days that never end.

Some nights you're breathing fire,
Some nights you're carved in ice.
Some nights are like nothing
I've ever seen before or ever will again.

Maybe I'm crazy,
But it's crazy and it's true.
I know you can save me.
No one else can save me now but you.

As long as the planets are turning,
As long as the stars are burning,
As long as your dreams are coming true,
You better believe it
That I would do anything for love.
Oh, I would do anything for love.
Oh, I would do anything for love,
But I won't do that.
No I won't do that.

Refrain:
I would do anything for love,
Anything you've been dreaming of,
But I just won't do that.

Repeat Refrain

Some days I pray for silence,
Some days I pray for soul.
Some days I just pray to the god
Of sex and drums and rock 'n' roll.

Maybe I'm lonely,
And that's all I'm qualified to be.
There's just one and only,
The one and only promise I can keep.
As long as the wheels are turning,
As long as the fires are burning,
As long as your prayers are coming true,
You better believe it
That I would do anything for love
And you know it's true and that's a fact.
I would do anything for love,
And there'll never be no turning back.
But I'll never do it better than I do it with you.
So long, so long.
And I would do anything for love.
Oh. I would do anything for love.

I would do anything for love,
But I won't do that,
No, no, no, I won't do that.

Girl:
Will you raise me up,
Will you help me down?
Will you get me tight out
Of the God forsaken town?
Will you make it all a little less cold?

Boy:
I can do that,
Oh, no I can do that.

Girl:
Will you cater to every fantasy I got?
Will you hose me down
With holy water if I get too hot?
Will you take me places I've never gone?

Boy:
I can do that,
Oh, no I can do that.

Girl:
I know the territory.
I've been around.
It'll all turn to dust
And we'll all fall down.
Sooner or later you'll be screwing around.

Boy:
I won't do that.
No, I won't do that.

Girl:
Anything for love,
But I won't do that.

If I Ever Lose My Faith in You

Music and Lyrics by Sting

recorded by Sting

You could say I lost my faith in science and progress.
You could say I lost my belief in the holy church.
You could say I lost my sense of direction.
You could say all of this and worse, but:

Refrain:
If I ever lose my faith in you
There'd be nothing left for me to do.
Some would say I was a lost man in a lost world.
You could say I lost my faith in the people on TV
You could say I lost my belief in our politicians.
They all seem like game show hosts to me.

Refrain

Hey, hey.
I could be lost inside their lies without a trace.
But every time I close my eyes I see your face.
I never saw no miracle of science
That didn't go from a blessing to a curse.
I never saw no military solution
That didn't always end up as something worse,
But, let me say this first:

If I ever lose my faith in you
If I ever lose my faith in you
There'd be nothing left for me to do.
There'd be nothing left for me to do.
If I ever lose my faith,
If I ever lose my faith,
If I ever lose my faith,
If I ever lose my faith in you...

I'll Be

Words and Music by Edwin McCain

recorded by Edwin McCain

The strands in your eyes
That color them wonderful
Stop me and steal my breath.
And emeralds from mountains
Thrust toward the sky,
Never revealing their depth.

Refrain 1:
And tell me that we belong together.
Dress it up with the trappings of love.
I'll be captivated,
I'll hang from your lips
Instead of the gallows of heartache
That hang from above.

Refrain 2:
I'll be your cryin' shoulder,
I'll be love suicide.
And I'll be better when I'm older,
I'll be the greatest fan of your life.

And rain falls angry on the tin roof
As we lie awake in my bed.
And you're my survival,
You're my living proof
My love is alive and not dead.

Refrain 1

Refrain 2

And I've dropped out, I've burned up.
I fought my way back from the dead.
I've tuned in, turned on, remembered the thing that you said.

Refrain 2 Twice

I'm the Only One

Words and Music by Melissa Etheridge

recorded by Melissa Etheridge

Please, baby, can't you see
My mind's a burnin' hell.
I got razors a-rippin' and tearin'
And strippin' my heart apart as well.
Tonight you told me
That you ache for something new,
And some other woman is lookin'
Like something that might be good for you.

Refrain:
Go on and hold her till
The screamin' is gone.
Go on, believe her
When she tells you nothing's wrong.
But I'm the only one
Who'll walk across the fire for you,
And I'm the only one
Who'll drown in my desire for you.
It's only fear that makes you run,
The demons that you're hidin' from.
When all your promises are gone,
I'm the only one.

Please, baby, can't you see
I'm tryin' to explain.
I've been here before and I'm lockin' the door
And I'm not goin' back again.
Her eyes and arms and skin
Won't make it go away.
You'll wake up tomorrow and wrestle
The sorrow that holds you down today.

Refrain Twice

Yeah, yeah.
And I'm the only one
Who'll drown in my desire for you.
It's only fear that makes you run,
The demons that you're hiding from.
When all your promises are gone,
I'm the only one.

If You Had My Love

Words and Music by Rodney Jerkins, LaShawn Daniels, Cory Rooney, Fred Jerkins
and Jennifer Lopez

recorded by Jennifer Lopez

Refrain:
If you had my love and I gave you all my trust
Would you comfort me?
And if somehow you knew
That your love would be untrue
Would you lie to me and call me "baby"?

Now if I give you me,
This is how it's got to be:
First of all, I won't take you cheating on me.
Tell me who can I trust if I can't trust in you?
And I refuse to let you play me for a fool.
You said, we could possibly spend eternity.
See, that's what you told me, that's what you said.
But if you want me you have to be fulfilling all my dreams.

You said you want my love and you've got to have it all.
But first there are some things you need to know.
If you wanna live with all I have to give
I need to feel true love or it's got to end, yeah.
I don't want you tryin' to get with me and I end up unhappy.
I don't need the hurt and I don't need the pain.
So before I do give myself to you,
I'll have to know the truth.
If I spend my life with you.

Refrain Three Times

Insensitive

Words and Music by Anne Loree

recorded by Jann Arden

How do you cool your lips after a summer's kiss?
How do you rid the sweat after the body bliss?
How do you turn your eyes from the romantic glare?
How do you block the sound of a voice you'd know anywhere?

Refrain:
Oh, I really should have known by the time you drove me home,
By the vagueness in your eyes, your casual goodbyes,
By the chill in your embrace, the expression on your face
That told me maybe you might have some advice to give
On how to be insensitive, insensitive, insensitive.

How do you numb your skin after the warmest touch?
How do you slow your blood after the body rush?
How do you free your soul after you've found a friend?
How do you teach your heart it's a crime to fall in love again?

Oh, you probably won't remember me, it's probably ancient history.
I'm one of the chosen few who went ahead and fell for you.
I'm out of vogue, I'm out of touch, I fell too fast, I feel too much.
I thought that you might have some advice to give
On how to be insensitive.

Refrain

The Impression That I Get

Words and Music by Dicky Barrett and Joe Gittleman

recorded by The Mighty Mighty Bosstones

Have you ever been close to tragedy
Or been close to folks who have?
Have you ever felt a pain so powerful,
So heavy you collapse?

Refrain:
I've never had to knock on wood,
But I know someone who has,
Which make me wonder if I could.
It makes me wonder if I've
Never had to knock on wood.
And I'm glad I haven't yet
Because I'm sure it isn't good.
That's the impression that I get.

Have you ever had the odds stacked up
So high you need a strength most don't possess?
Or has it ever come down to do or die?
You've got to rise above the rest.

Refrain

I'm not a coward. I've just never been tested.
I'd like to think that if I was, I would pass.
Look at the tested and think there but for the grace go.
I might be a coward, I'm afraid of what I might find out.

Refrain

I've never had, I'd better knock on wood
'Cause I know someone who has,
Which make me wonder if I could.
It makes me wonder if I never had,
I'd better knock on wood
'Cause I'm sure it isn't good,
And I'm glad I haven't yet.
That's the impression that I get.

Iris

Words and Music by John Rzeznik

from the Motion Picture *City of Angels*
recorded by Goo Goo Dolls

And I'd give up forever to touch you
'Cause I know that you feel me somehow.
You're the closest to heaven that I'll ever be
And I don't wanna go home right now.

And all I could taste is this moment,
And all I can breathe is your life.
And sooner or later it's over.
I just don't wanna miss you tonight.

Refrain:
And I don't want the world to see me
'Cause I don't think that they'd understand.
When everything's made to be broken
I just want you to know who I am.

And you can't fight the tears that ain't coming,
Or the moment of truth in your lies.
When everything feels like the movies,
Yeah, you bleed just to know you're alive.

Refrain Twice

It's All Coming Back to Me Now

Words and Music by Jim Steinman

recorded by Celine Dion

There were nights when the wind was so cold
That my body froze in bed
If I just listened to it right outside the window.
There were days when the sun was so cruel,
All the tears turned to dust,
And I just knew my eyes were drying out forever.

I finished crying in the instant that you left,
And I can't remember where or when or how.
And I banished every memory you and I had ever made.

But when you touch me like this,
And you kiss me like that,
I just have to admit that it's all coming back to me.
When I touch you like this,
And I hold you like that,
It's so hard to believe, but it's all coming back to me.
(It's all coming back, it's all coming back to me now.)

There were moments of gold,
And there were flashes of light,
There were things I'd never do again,
But then they'd always seemed right.
There were nights of endless pleasure.
It was more than any lovers in love.

Baby, baby if I kiss you like this,
And if you whisper like that,
It was lost long ago, but that's all coming back to me.
If you want me like this,
And if you want me like that,
It was that long ago, but it's all coming back to me.
It's so hard to resist, and it's all coming back to me.
I can barely recall, but it's all coming back to me now.

Thought you were history with the slamming of the door,
And I made myself so strong again somehow.
And I never wasted any of my time on you since then.

But if I touch you like this,
And if you kiss me like that,
It was so long ago, but it's all coming back to me.
If you touch me like this,
And if I kiss you like that,
It was gone with the wind, but it's all coming back to me.
(It's all coming back, it's all coming back to me now.)

There were moments of gold,
And there were flashes of light.
There were things we'd never do again,
But then they'd always seemed right.
There were nights of endless pleasure.
It was more that all your lovers in love.

Baby, baby, baby, when you touch me like this,
And when you hold me like that,
It was gone with the wind, but it's all coming back to me.
When you see me like this,
And when I see you like that,
Then we've seen what we want to see, all coming back to me.
The flesh and the fantasies all coming back to me.
I can barely recall, but it's all coming back to me now.

If you forgive me all this,
If I forgive you all that,
We forgive and forget, and it's all coming back to me now
(It's all coming back to me now.)
And when I touch you like that. (It's all coming back to me now.)
And if you do it like this. (It's all coming back to me now.)

Ironic

Lyrics by Alanis Morissette
Music by Alanis Morissette and Glen Ballard

recorded by Alanis Morissette

An old man turned ninety-eight.
He won the lottery, and died the next day.
It's a black fly in your Chardonnay.
It's a death row pardon two minutes too late.

Refrain:
Isn't it ironic… don't you think?
It's like rain on your wedding day.
It's a free ride when you're already paid.
It's the good advice that you didn't take.
Who would've thought… it figures.

Mister Play It Safe was afraid to fly.
He packed his suitcase and kissed his kids goodbye.
He waited his whole damn life to take that flight,
And as the plane crashed down, he thought,
"Well, isn't this nice…"

Refrain

Well, life has a funny way of sneaking up on you
When you think everything's O.K. and everything's going right.
And life has a funny way of helping you out
When you think everything's gone wrong
And everything blows up in your face.

A traffic jam when you're already late.
A no smoking sign on your cigarette break.
It's like ten thousand spoons when all you need is a knife.
It's meeting the man of my dreams,
And then meeting his beautiful wife.

Isn't it ironic... don't you think?
A little too ironic... and yeah, I really do think...
It's like rain on your wedding day.
It's a free ride when you're already paid.
It's the good advice that you didn't take.
And who would've thought, it figures.
And you know life has a funny way of sneaking up on you.
Life has a funny, funny way of helping you out,
Helping you out.

It's All About the Benjamins

Words and Music by Sean "Puffy" Combs, Notorious B.I.G., Sean Jacobs,
 Jason Phillips, David Styles, Deric Angelettie and Kim Jones

Recorded by Puff Daddy & The Family

Uhh, uh-huh, yeah.
Uhh, uh-huh, yeah.
It's all about the Benjamins, baby.
Uhh, uh-huh, yeah.
It's all about the Benjamins, baby.
Goodfellas, uhh.

Puff Daddy:
Now, what y'all wanna do?
Wanna be ballers? Shot callers?
Brawlers who be dippin' in the Benz wit' the spoilers
On the low from the Jake in the Taurus,
Tryin' to get my hands on some Grants like Horace.
Yeah, livin' the raw deal, three-course meals:
Spaghetti, fettuccini, and veal.
But still, everything's real in the field
And what you can't have now, leave in your will.
But don't knock me for tryin' to bury
Seven zeros over in Rio de Janier-y.
Ain't nobody's hero, but I wanna be heard
On your Hot 9–7 every day, that's my word.
Swimmin' in women wit' they own condominiums.
Five plus fives, who drive Milleniums.

It's all about the Benjamins—what?
I get a fifty-pound bag of ooh for the mutts.
Five carats on my hand wit' the cuts
And swim in European figures.
Fuck bein' a broke nigga.

Jadakiss:
I want-a all chromed out wit' the clutch, nigga.
Drinkin' malt liquor, drivin' a Bro' Vega.
I'm wit' Mo' sippers, watched by gold-diggers, (Uhh.)
Rockin' Bejor denims wit' gold zippers. (C'mon.)
Lost your touch, we kept ours, poppin' Cristals,
Freakin' the three-quarter reptiles. (Ahahah.)
Enormous cream, forest green Benz jeep
For my team, so while you sleep, I'm-a scheme. (That's right.)
We see through, that's why nobody never gon' believe you.
You should do what we do: stack slips like Hebrews.
Don't let the melody intrigue you (Uh-huh.)
'Cause I leave you, I'm only here
for that green paper with the eagle.

Sheek:
I'm strictly tryin' to cop those colossal-sized Picassos
And have pappy flip coke outside Delgado's. (Whoo!)
Mienda, with cash flowin' like Sosa
And the Latin chick transportin' in the chocha.
Stampedin' over, pop Mo's, never sober,
Lex and Range Rovers, dealin' weight by Minnesota. (Uhh.)
Avoidin' narcs wit' camcorders and Chevy Novas, (Uh-huh.)
Stash in the buildin' wit' this chick named Alona (Uh-huh.)
From Daytona, when I was young I wants to bone her. (Uh-huh.)
But now I only hit chicks that win beauty pageants. (Ahahaha.)
Trickin', they takin' me skiing at the Aspens. (C'mon.)
Uhh, gangsta mental, stay poppin' Cristal,
Pack a black pistol in the Ac' Coupe that's dark brown. (Whoo!)
Pinky-ringin', gondolas wit' the man singin',
Italian music down the river wit' your chick clingin'
To my bizzalls; player, you mad false,
Actin' hard when you as pussy as RuPaul.

Puff Daddy:
C'mon, c'mon, uh-huh.
It's all about the Benjamins, baby,
Uh-huh, yeah.
It's all about the Benjamins, baby,
Uh-huh, yeah.
It's all about the Benjamins, baby,
Uh-huh, yeah.
It's all about the Benjamins, baby,
Uh-huh, yeah.
It's all about the Benjamins, baby,
Now what y'all wanna do?
It's all about the Benjamins, baby,
Wanna be ballers, shot callers?
It's all about the Benjamins, baby,
Brawlers, who be dippin' in the Benz wit' the spoilers.
It's all about the Benjamins, baby,
On the low from the Jake in the Taurus.

Lil' Kim:
Uhh, uhh, what the blood clot?
Wanna bumble wit' the Bee, hah?
Bzzzt, throw a hex on a whole family. (Yeah, yeah, yeah.)
Dressed in all black like the Oman. (Say what?)
Have your friends singin' "This is for my homie." (That's right.)
And you know me, from makin' niggaz so sick,
Floss in my six with the Lex on the wrist.
If it's Murder, you know She Wrote it, (Uh-huh.)
German Luger for your ass bitch, deep throated.
Know you wanna fill the room 'cause it's platinum-coated.
Take your pick, got a firearm you should o' toted.
Suck a dick, all that bullshit you kick,
Playa hatin' from the sideline, get your own shit.
Why you ridin' mine? (Uh-huh.)

I'm a Goodfella kinda lady,
Stash 380s and Mercedes,
Puffy, hold me down, baby!
Only female in my crew, and I kick shit
Like a nigga do, with a trigga, too, fuck you.

Notorious B.I.G.:
Yeah, yeah, uhh, uhh, uhh!
I been had skills, Cristal spills,
Hide bills in Brazil, about a mil' to ice grill.
Make it hard to figure me, liquor be kickin' me
In my asshole, uhh, undercover, Donnie Brasco
Lent my East Coast girl the Bentley to twirl, (Uh-huh.)
My West Coast shorty, push the chrome, seven-forty.
Rockin' Redman and Naughty, all in my kitty-kat,
Half a brick of yeah, in the bra where her titties at.
And I'm livin' that, whole life, we push weight. (Uh-huh.)
Fuck the state pen, fuck hoes at Penn State. (C'mon.)
Listen close, it's Francis, the Praying Mantis,
Grip on the whip for the smooth getaway.
Playa haters get away or my lead will spray.
Squeeze off 'til I'm empty—don't tempt me.
Only, to Hell I send thee, all about the Benjis.
What?

Puff Daddy:
It's all about the Benjamins, baby,
Uh-huh, yeah.

Jane Says

Words and Music by Perry Farrell, Dave Navarro, Stephen Perkins and Eric Avery

recorded by Jane's Addiction

Jane says, "I'm done with Sergio; he treat me like a rag doll."
She hides her television.
Says, "I don't owe him nothing. But if he comes back again,
Tell him to wait right here for me or try again tomorrow."
"I'm gonna kick tomorrow. I'm gonna kick tomorrow."

Jane says, "Have you seen my wig around? I feel naked without it."
She knows they all want her to go.
But that's okay; man, she don't like them anyway.
Jane says, "I'm going away to Spain when I get my money saved.
Gonna start tomorrow."
"I'm gonna kick tomorrow. I'm gonna kick tomorrow."

She gets mad and she starts to cry.
She takes a swing, man. She can't hit!
She don't mean no harm; she just don't know
What else to do about it.

But Jane goes to the store at eight; she walks up on St. Andrews.
She waits and a gets her dinner there.
She pulls her dinner from her pocket.
Jane says, "I ain't never been in love; I don't know what it is."
She only knows if someone wants her.

"I want 'em if they want me. I only know they want me."
She gets mad and she starts to cry.
She takes a swing, She can't hit!
She don't mean no harm; she just don't know
What else to do about it.

Jane says…
Jane says…
Ah. Hoo, hoo, hoo, hoo, hoo, hoo, hoo.

Jeremy

Music by Jeff Ament
Lyric by Eddie Vedder

recorded by Pearl Jam

At home drawing pictures of mountain tops, with him on top.
Lemon yellow sun; arms raised in a V.
The dead lay in pools of maroon below.
Daddy didn't give attention, oh,
To the fact that Mommy didn't care.
King Jeremy the wicked oh, ruled his world.
Jeremy spoke in class today. Jeremy spoke in class today.

Clearly I remember picking on the boy, seemed a harmless little fuck.
Ooh, but we unleashed a lion.
Gnashed his teeth and bit the recess lady's breast.
How could I forget?
And he hit me with a surprise, left my jaw left hurtin',
Ooh, dropped wide open. Just like the day, oh, like the day I heard
Daddy didn't give affection, no,
And the boy was something that Mommy wouldn't wear.
King Jeremy the wicked, oh, ruled his world.
Jeremy spoke in class today. Jeremy spoke in class today.
Jeremy spoke in class today.
Try to forget this. Try to erase this from the black.

Jeremy spoke in class today. Jeremy spoke in class today.
Jeremy spoke in class today. Jeremy spoke in, spoke in,
Jeremy spoke in, spoke in.

Repeat Nine Times:
Jeremy spoke in class today.

Ah-ha, ah-ha, ah-ha, ah-ha.

The Keeper of the Stars

Words and Music by Karen Staley, Danny Mayo and Dickey Lee

recorded by Tracy Byrd

It was no accident, me finding you.
Someone had a hand in it long before we ever knew.
Now I just can't believe you're in my life.
Heaven's smiling down on me as I look at you tonight.

I tip my hat to the keeper of the stars.
He sure knew what he was doin'
When he joined these two hearts.
I hold everything when I hold you in my arms.
I've got all I'll ever need, thanks to the keeper of the stars.

Soft moonlight on your face, oh, how you shine.
It takes my breath away just to look into your eyes.
I know I don't deserve a treasure like you.
There really are no words to show my gratitude.

So I tip my hat to the keeper of the stars.
He sure knew what he was doin'
When he joined these two hearts.
I hold everything when I hold you in my arms.
I've got all I'll ever need, thanks to the keeper of the stars.

It was no accident, me finding you.
Someone had a hand in it long before we ever knew.

Jesus He Knows Me

Words and Music by Tony Banks, Phil Collins and Mike Rutherford

recorded by Genesis

D'you see the face on the TV screen,
Coming at you every Sunday.
See the face on the billboard, well, that man is me.
On the cover of the magazine,
There's no question why I'm smiling.
You buy a piece of paradise, you buy a piece of me.
I'll get you everything you wanted,
I'll get you everything you need.
You don't need to believe in hereafter,
Just believe in me.

Refrain:
'Cause Jesus, he knows me and he knows I'm right.
I've been talking to Jesus all my life.
Oh yes, he knows me and he knows I'm right.
And he's been telling me everything is all right.

I believe in the family,
With my ever loving wife beside me.
But she don't know about my girlfriend
Or the man I met last night.
Do you believe in God? 'Cause that is what I'm selling.
And if you wanna get to heaven, I'll see you right.
You won't even have to leave your house
Or get out of your chair.
You don't even have to touch that dial
'Cause I'm everywhere.

Refrain

Won't find me practicing what I'm preaching.
Won't find me making no sacrifice.
But I can get you a pocketful of miracles,
If you promise to be good, try to be nice.
God will take good care of you
But just do as I say, don't do as I do.

Well, I'm counting my blessings
'Cause I've found true happiness.
'Cause I'm getting richer, day by day.
You can find me in the phone book,
Just call my toll-free number.
You can do it any way you want
Just do it right away.
And there'll be no doubt in your mind,
You'll believe everything I'm saying.
If you wanna get closer to him,
Get on your knees and start paying.

Refrain

'Cause Jesus, he knows me and he knows I'm right.
(And Jesus, he knows me, you know.)
Ooh yes, he knows me and he knows I'm right.
(Jesus, he knows me, you know.)
I've been talking to Jesus all my life
And he's been telling me
Everything's gonna be alright, alright.
Jesus, he knows me, Jesus, he knows me, you know.

Repeat and Fade:
Jesus, he knows me, Jesus, he knows me, you know.

King of Wishful Thinking

Words and Music by Martin Page, Peter Cox and Richard Drummie

from the Motion Picture *Pretty Woman*
recorded by Go West

I don't need to fall at your feet
Just 'cause you cut me to the bone.
And I won't miss the way that you kiss me.
We were never carved in stone.
If I don't listen to the talk of the town,
Maybe I can fool myself.

Refrain:
And I'll get over you, I know I will.
I'll pretend my ship's not sinking.
And I'll tell myself I'm over you,
'Cause I'm the king of wishful thinking.
I am the king of wishful thinking.

I refuse to give in to my blues.
That's not how it's gonna be.
And I deny the tears in my eyes.
I don't want to let you see, no,
That you have made a hole in my heart.
And now I've got to fool myself.

Refrain

If I don't listen to the talk of the town,
Maybe I can fool myself.

Refrain

Repeat and Fade:
I'll get over you, I know I will.
You made a hole in my heart,
But I won't shed a tear for you.
I'll be the king of wishful thinking.

Learning to Fly

Words and Music by Jeff Lynne and Tom Petty

recorded by Tom Petty

Well, I started out down a dirty road,
Started out all alone.
And the sun went down as I crossed the hill,
And the town lit up, the world got still.
I'm learning to fly, but I ain't got wings.
Coming down is the hardest thing.

Well, the good ol' days may not return,
And the rocks might melt and the sea may burn.
I'm learning to fly around the clouds.
What goes up must come down.

Well, some say life will beat you down
And break your heart, steal your crown.
So I started out for God knows where.
I guess I'll know when I get there.
I'm learning to fly, but I ain't got wings.
Coming down is the hardest thing.

I'm learning to fly around the clouds.
What goes up must come down.
I'm learning to fly.
I'm learning to fly.

Lightning Crashes

Words and Music by Edward Kowalczyk, Chad Taylor, Patrick Dahlheimer
and Chad Gracey

recorded by Live

Lightning crashes, a new mother cries.
Her placenta falls to the floor.
The angel opens her eyes. The confusion sets in,
Before the doctor can even close the door.

Lightning crashes, and old mother dies.
Her intentions fall to the floor.
The angel closes her eyes. The confusion that was hers,
Belongs now, to the baby down the hall.

Refrain:
Oh, now feel it comin' back again
Like a rollin' thunder chasing the wind.
Forces pullin' from the center of the Earth again.
I can feel it.

Lightning crashes, a new mother cries.
This moment she's been waiting for.
The angel opens her eyes, a pale blue colored iris,
Presents the circle, and puts the glory out to hide.

Refrain Three Times

Yeah, I can feel it,
Yeah, I can feel it, yeah.

Let Her Cry

Words and Music by Darius Carlos Rucker, Everett Dean Felber, Mark William Bryan
and James George Sonefeld

recorded by Hootie & the Blowfish

She sits alone by a lamppost
Tryin' to find a thought that's escaped her mind.
She says, "Dad's the one I love the most,
But Stipe's not far behind."

She never lets me in, only tells me where she's been
When she's had too much to drink.
I say that I don't care,
I just run my hands through her dark hair,
And I pray to God, you gotta help me fly away. And just

Refrain:
Let her cry, if the tears fall down like rain.
Let her sing if it eases all her pain.
Let her go, let her walk right out on me.
And if the sun comes up tomorrow, let her be, let her be.

This morning I woke up alone, found a note standing by the phone
Sayin', "Maybe, maybe I'll be back some day."
I wanted to look for you, you walked in.
I didn't know just what to do,
So I sat back down, had a beer and felt sorry for myself. Sayin'

Refrain

Last night I tried to leave, cried so much, I could not believe
She was the same girl I fell in love with long ago.
She went in the back to get high.
I sat down on my couch and cried,
Yelling, "Oh, mama, please help me. Won't you hold my hand?" And

Refrain

Life Is a Highway

Words and Music by Tom Cochrane

recorded by Tom Cochrane

Life's like a road that you travel on
When there's one day here and the next day gone.
Sometimes you bend and sometimes you stand.
Sometimes you turn your back to the wind.
There's a world outside every darkened door
Where blues won't haunt you anymore.
Where the brave are free and lovers soar,
Come ride with me to the distant shore.
We won't hesitate. Break down the garden gate.
There's not much time left today.

Refrain:
Life is a highway.
I wanna ride it all night long.
If you're going my way,
I wanna drive it all night long.

Through all these cities and all these towns,
It's in my blood and it's all around.
I love you now like I loved you then.
This is the road and these are the hands.
From Mozambique to those Memphis nights,
The Khyber pass to Vancouver's lights.
Knock me down, get back up again,
You're in my blood. I'm not a lonely man.
There's no load I can't hold. Road so rough, this I know.
I'll be there when the light comes in.
Just tell 'em we're survivors.

Refrain Twice

There was a distance between you and I.
A misunderstanding once, but now we look it in the eye.
Oh. Mm. There ain't no load that I can't hold.
Road so rough, this I know.
I'll be there when the light comes in.
Just tell 'em we're survivors.

Refrain

Linger

Lyrics by Dolores O'Riordan
Music by Dolores O'Riordan and Noel Hogan

recorded by The Cranberries

If you, if you could return,
Don't let it burn, don't let it fade.
I'm sure I'm not being rude,
But it's just your attitude.
It's tearing me apart,
It's ruining everything.

I swore, I swore I would be true,
And honey, so did you.
So why were you holding her hand?
Is that the way we stand?
Were you lying all the time?
Was it just a game to you?

Refrain:
But I'm in so deep
You know I'm such a fool for you.
You got me wrapped around your finger, ah, ha, ha.
Do you have to let it linger?
Do you have to, do you have to,
Do you have to let it linger?

Oh, I thought the world of you.
I thought nothing could go wrong,
But I was wrong. I was wrong.

If you, if you could get by
Trying not to lie,
Things wouldn't be so confused
And I wouldn't feel so used,
But you always really knew
I just wanna be with you.

Refrain Twice

You know I'm such a fool for you.
You got me wrapped around your finger, ah, ha, ha.
Do you have to let it linger?
Do you have to, do you have to,
Do you have to let it linger?

Little Miss Can't Be Wrong

Words and Music by Spin Doctors

recorded by Spin Doctors

Uh, been a whole lot easier since the bitch left town.
I been a whole lot happier without her face around.
Nobody upstairs uh, gonna stomp and shout.
Nobody at the back door gonna throw my laundry out.
She hold the shotgun while you do-si-so.
She want one man made of Hercules and Cyrano.
Been a whole lot easier since the bitch is gone.
Little miss, little miss, little miss can't be wrong.

Refrain:
Little miss, little miss, little miss can't be wrong,
Ain't nobody gonna bow no more when you sound your gong.
Little miss, little miss, little miss can't be wrong.
What you go'n do, get into another one of these here rock 'n roll songs?

Other people's thoughts, they ain't your hand-me-downs.
Would it be so bad to simply turn around?
You cook so well, all nice and French.
You do your brain surgery too, mama, with a monkey wrench.

Refrain

Yeah. Can't be wrong.
Yeah. Can't be wrong.
Yeah. Can't be wrong.
Yeah. Can't be wrong.

I hope them cigarettes are gonna make you cough.
I hope you heard this song, and it pissed you off.
I take that back, I hope you're doin' fine.
And if I had a dollar, I'd maybe give you ninety-nine.

Refrain Twice

Little miss, little miss, little miss can't be wrong. Oh,
Ain't nobody gonna bow no more when you sound your gong.
Yeah, little miss, little miss, little miss can't be wrong. Oh,
What ya go'n do, baby? What ya go'n do, baby?
Oh, ya can't be wrong; you darling can't be wrong.
Can't be wrong yeah, oh, oh, oh, yeah, yeah, yeah, you can't.

Livin' La Vida Loca

Words and Music by Robi Rosa and Desmond Child

recorded by Ricky Martin

She's into superstitions.
Black cats and voodoo dolls.
I feel a premonition.
That girl's gonna make me fall.

She's into new sensations,
New kicks in the candlelight.
She's got a new addiction
For every day and night.

She'll make you take your clothes off
And go dancing in the rain.
She'll make you live her crazy life,
But she'll take away your pain
Like a bullet to your brain.

Refrain:
Upside inside out,
She's livin' la vida loca.
She'll push and pull you down
Livin' la vida loca.
Her lips are devil red
And her skin's the color of mocha.
She will wear you out
Livin' la vida loca.

You're livin' la vida loca.
She's livin' la vida loca.

Wake up in New York City
In a funky cheap hotel.
She took my heart and she took my money.
She must've slipped me a sleepin' pill.

She never drinks the water
And makes you order French champagne.
Once you've had a taste of her
You'll never be the same.
Yeah, she'll make you go insane.

Refrain

You're livin' la vida loca.
She's livin' la vida loca.

She'll make you take your clothes off
And go dancing in the rain.
She'll make you live her crazy life,
But she'll take away your pain
Like a bullet to your brain.

Refrain Twice

You're livin' la vida loca.
She's livin la vida loca.

Livin' la vida loca.
A-gotta, gotta, gotta la vida loca.
Gotta, gotta, gotta la vida loca.

Loser

Words by Beck Hansen
Music by Beck Hansen and Karl Stephenson

recorded by Beck

Rap:
In the time of chimpanzees, I was a monkey
Butane in my veins and a mouth to cut the junkies with the
plastic eyeballs.
Spray paint the vegetables. Dog food skulls with the beefcake
pantyhose.
Kill the headlights and put it in neutral.
Got a couple of couches. Stockcar flaming with the loser and the
    cruise control.
Baby's in Reno with the vitamin D. Got a couple of couches
Asleep on the love seat.
Someone keeps saying I'm insane to complain about a
    shotgun wedding
And a stain on my shirt.
Don't believe everything that you breathe.
You get a parking violation and a maggot on your sleeve.
So shave your face with some mace in the dark
Saving all your food stamps and burning down the trailer park.
Bent all the music with the phony gas chamber.
Yo, cut it.

Refrain (sung):
Soy un perdidor. I'm a loser, baby.
So, why don't you kill me?
Soy un perdidor. I'm a loser, baby,
So, why don't you kill me?

Rap:
Forces of evil and a bozo nightmare.
'Cause one's got a weasel and another's got a flag.
One's on the pole. Shove the other in a bag with the rerun shows.
And the cocaine nose job, the daytime crap of the folk singer slob.
He hung himself with guitar string.
A slab of turkey neck and it's hangin' from a pigeon wing.
So get right if you can't relate. Trade the cash for the beef
For the body for the hate.
And my time is a piece of wax falling on a termite
Who's choking on the splinters.

Refrain

Spoken: Drive by body pierce.

Refrain

(Can't Live Without Your) Love and Affection

Words and Music by Marc Tanner, Matt Nelson and Gunnar Nelson

recorded by Nelson

Here she comes, mm, just like an angel.
Seems like forever that she's been on my mind.
Nothing has changed, she thinks I'm a waste of her time.

There she goes. No, she don't know what she's missing.
Can't she see I'll never give up the fight.
I'll do all I can. She understands my desire.

I've been on the outside looking in.
Let me into your heart, oh.
There's nothing on earth that should keep us apart.

Baby, I can't live without your love and affection.
I can't face another night on my own.
I'd give up my pride to save me from being alone,
'Cause I can't live without your love. Ooh, your love.

So I wait, mm, here for an answer.
Wonder if tomorrow will be like this today.
I keep holding on, can't go on living this way, baby.

I've been on the outside looking in.
Bring my tears to an end, oh.
I realize it's no use for me to pretend.

Oh, yeah, I can't live without your love and affection.
I can't face another night on my own.
I'd give up my pride to save me from being alone,
'Cause I can't live without your love.

With your love, I put my arms around you.
Can't find the words to tell you
That I can't live without your love.

I can't live without your love and affection.
I can't face another night on my own.
I'd give up my pride to save me from being alone.

Baby, I can't live without your love and affection.
I just can't go on this way anymore.
As hard as I try there's one thing that I know for sure.
I can't live without your love.

Repeat and Fade:
There she goes.
I can't live without your love, baby.

Love of a Lifetime

Words and Music by Bill Leverty and Carl Snare

recorded by Firehouse

I guess the time was right for us to say
We'd take our time and live our lives together day by day.
We'll make a wish and send it on a prayer.
We know our dreams can all come true,
With love that we can share.

With you I never wonder,
"Will you be there for me?"
With you I never wonder.
You're the right one for me.

Refrain:
I finally found the love of a lifetime,
A love to last my whole life through.
I finally found the love of a lifetime forever in my heart.
I finally found the love of a lifetime.

With every kiss, our love is like brand new
And every star up in the sky was made for me and you.
Still, we both know that the road is long,
But we know that we will be together
Because our love is strong.

Refrain Twice

I finally found the love of a lifetime...

Love Will Keep Us Alive

Words and Music by Peter Vale, Jim Capaldi and Paul Carrack

recorded by Eagles

I was standing, all alone against the world outside.
You were searching for a place to hide.
Lost and lonely, now you've given me the will to survive.
When we're hungry, love will keep us alive.

Don't you worry, sometimes you've just got to let it ride.
The world is changing right before your eyes.
Now I've found you, there's no more emptiness inside.
When we're hungry, love will keep us alive.

I would die for you, climb the highest mountain.
Baby, there's nothing I wouldn't do.

Now I've found you, there's no more emptiness inside.
When we're hungry love will keep us alive.

I would die for you, climb the highest mountain.
Baby, there's nothing I wouldn't do.

I was standing, all alone against the world outside.
You were searching for a place to hide.
Lost and lonely, now you've given me the will to survive.
When we're hungry, love will keep us alive.

When we're hungry, love will keep us alive.
When we're hungry, love will keep us alive.

Lovefool

Music by Peter Svensson
Lyrics by Nina Persson and Peter Svensson

recorded by The Cardigans

Dear, I fear we're facing a problem.
You love me no longer, I know,
And maybe there is nothing
That I can do to make you do.
Mama tells me I shouldn't bother,
That I ought to stick to another man,
A man that surely deserves me.
But I think you do.

Refrain:
So I cry and I pray and I beg.
Love me, love me, say that you love me.
Fool me, fool me, go on and fool me.
Love me, love me, pretend that you love me.
Leave me, leave me, just say that you need me.
So I cry and I beg for you to love me, love me.
Say that you love me.
Leave me, leave me, just say that you need me.
I can't care about anything but you.

Lately I have desp'rately pondered.
Spent my nights awake and I wonder
What I could have done in another way
To make you stay.
Reason will not lead to solution.
I will end up lost in confusion.
I don't care if you really care
As long as you don't go.

Refrain

Love me, love me, say that you love me.
Fool me, fool me, go on and fool me.
Love me, love me. I know that you need me.
I can't care about anything but you.

Mama, I'm Coming Home

Words and Music by Ozzy Osbourne and Zakk Wylde

recorded by Ozzy Osbourne

Times have changed and times are strange.
Here I come, but I ain't the same.
Mama, I'm coming home.
Time's gone by. Seems to be
You could have been a better friend to me.
Mama, I'm coming home.

You took me in and you drove me out, yeah.
You had me hypnotized, yeah,
Lost and found and turned around
By the fire in your eyes.

You made me cry, you told me lies,
But I can't stand to say goodbye.
Mama, I'm coming home.
I could be right, I could be wrong.
It hurts so bad, it's been so long.
Mama, I'm coning home.

Selfish love, yeah, we're both alone,
The ride before the fall, yeah,
But, I'm gonna take this heart of stone.
I just got to have it all.
I've seen your face a hundred times
Every day we've been apart.

I don't care about the sunshine, yeah,
'Cause Mama, Mama, I'm coming home.
I'm coming home.

You took me in and you drove me out, yeah.
You had me hypnotized, yeah,
Lost and found and turned around
By the fire in your eyes.
I've seen your face a thousand times
Every day we've been apart.

I don't care about the sunshine, yeah,
'Cause Mama, Mama, I'm coming home.
I'm coming home. I'm coming home.
I'm coming home.

Mr. Jones

Words by Adam Duritz
Music by Adam Duritz and David Bryson

recorded by Counting Crows

Sha la la la la la la. Uh huh.
I was down at the New Amsterdam
Staring at this yellow-haired girl.
Mister Jones strikes up a conversation
With this black-haired flamenco dancer.
You know, she dances while his father plays guitar.
She's suddenly beautiful.
Well, we all want something beautiful.
Man, I wish I was beautiful.
So, come dance this silence down through the morning.
Sha la la la la la la la, yeah. Uh huh, yeah.

Cut up, Maria!
Show me some of them Spanish dances.
Pass me a bottle, Mister Jones.
Believe in me. Help me believe in anything
'Cause I want to be someone who believes. Yeah.
Mister Jones and me tell each other fairy tales
And we stare at the beautiful women.
"She's looking at you. Ah, no, she's looking at me."
Smiling in the bright lights, coming through in stereo.
When everybody loves you, you can never be lonely.

Well, I will paint my picture,
Paint myself in blue and red and black and gray.
All of the beautiful colors are very, very meaningful.
Yeah, well you know gray is my fav'rite color.

I felt so symbolic yesterday.
If I knew Picasso I would buy myself a gray guitar and play.
Mister Jones and me look into the future
And we stare at the beautiful women.
"She's looking at you. Oh, I don't think so.
She's looking at me."
Standing in the spotlight, I bought myself a gray guitar.
When everybody loves me, I will never be lonely.
I will never be lonely. Said, I'm never gonna be lonely.

I want to be a lion.
Yeah, everybody wants to pass as cats.
We all want to be big, big stars,
Yeah, but, we got different reasons for that.
Believe in me because I don't believe in anything
And I want to be someone to believe,
To believe, to believe, yeah.

Mister Jones and me stumbling through the bario.
Yeah, we stare at the beautiful women.
"She's perfect for you. Man, there's got to be somebody for me."
I want to be Bob Dylan.
Mister Jones wishes he was someone just a little more funky.
Where everybody loves you, ah, son,
That's just about as funky as you can be.

Mister Jones and me staring at the video.
When I look at the television
I want to see me staring right back at me.
We all want to be big stars,
But we don't know why and we don't know how.
But when everybody loves me,
I'm going to be just about as happy as I can be.

Mister Jones and me, we're gonna be big stars…

More Than Words

Words and Music by Nuno Bettencourt and Gary Cherone

recorded by Extreme

Sayin', "I love you"
Is not the words I want to hear from you.
It's not that I want you not to say.
But if you only knew how easy it would be,
To show me how you feel,
More than words is all you have to do to make it real.
Then you wouldn't have to say that you love me,
'Cause I'd already know.

Refrain:
What would you do if my heart was torn in two?
More than words to show you feel
That your love for me is real.
What would you say if I took those words away?
Then you couldn't make things new
Just by sayin', "I love you."

La di da da di da...
More than words.

Now that I have tried to talk to you
And make you understand.
All you have to do is close your eyes
And just reach out your hands.
And touch me, hold me close, don't ever let me go.

More than words is all I ever needed you to show.
Then you wouldn't have to say
That you love me,
'Cause I'd already know.

Refrain

More than words.

My Heart Will Go On
(Love Theme from 'Titanic')

Music by James Horner
Lyric by Will Jennings

from the Paramount and Twentieth Century Fox Motion Picture *Titanic*
recorded by Celine Dion

Every night in my dreams I see you, I feel you.
That is how I know you go on.
Far across the distance and spaces between us
You have come to show you go on.

Refrain:
Near, far, wherever you are,
I believe that the heart does go on.
Once more you open the door
And you're here in my heart,
And my heart will go on and on.

Love can touch us one time
And last for a lifetime,
And never let go till we're gone.
Love was when I loved you;
One true time I hold to.
In my life we'll always go on.

Refrain

You're here, there's nothing I fear
And I know that my heart will go on.
We'll stay forever this way.
You are safe in my heart,
And my heart will go on and on.

No Rain

Words and Music by Blind Melon

recorded by Blind Melon

All I can say is that my life is pretty plain,
I like watchin' the puddles gather rain.
And all I can do is just pour some tea for two
And speak my point of view but it's not sane.
It's not sane.

I just want someone to say to me, oh,
I'll always be there when you wake, yeah.
You know I'd like to keep my cheeks dry today.
So stay with me and I'll have it made.

And I don't understand why I sleep all day
And I start to complain that there's no rain.
And all I can do is read a book to stay awake,
And it rips my life away but it's a great escape.
Escape, escape, escape.

All I can say is that my life is pretty plain,
You don't like my point of view,
You think that I'm insane.
It's not sane, it's not sane.

I just want someone to say to me, oh,
I'll always be there when you wake, yeah.
You know I'd like to keep my cheeks dry today.
So stay with me and I'll have it made.
Oh. Oh. Oh.

My Own Worst Enemy

Words and Music by Jeremy Popoff, Jay Popoff, Kevin Baldes and
  Allen Shellenberger

recorded by Lit

Can we forget about the things I said
When I was drunk?
I didn't mean to call you that.
I can't remember what was said
Or what you threw at me.
Please tell me.

Refrain:
Please tell me why my car is in the front yard
And I'm sleeping with my clothes on.
I came in through the window last night
And you're gone. Gone.

It's no surprise to me;
I am my own worst enemy.
'Cause every now and then I kick
The living shit out of me.
The smoke alarm is going off
And there's a cigarette still burning.

Refrain

Please tell me why my car is in the front yard
And I'm sleeping with my clothes on.
I came in through the window last night.

Ah ooh. It's no surprise to me;
I am my own worst enemy.
Ah ooh. 'Cause every now and then
I kick the living shit out of me.
Ah ooh. Can we forget about the things I said
When I was drunk? Ah ooh.
I didn't mean to call you that.

Name

Words and Music by John Rzeznik

recorded by Goo Goo Dolls

And even though the moment passed me by,
I still can't turn away.
I saw the dreams you never thought you'd lose
Get tossed along the way.

And letters that you never meant to send
Get lost or thrown away.
And now I called up orphans,
I never knew their names,
Who don't belong to no one.
That's a shame.

You could hide beside me, maybe for awhile,
And I won't tell no one your name.
And I won't tell 'em your name.

The scars are souvenirs you never lose,
The past is never far.
And did you lose yourself somewhere out there?
Did you get to be a star?

And don't it make you sad to know that life
Is more than who we are?
You grew up way too fast
And now there's nothing to believe.
And reruns all become our history.

A tired song keeps playing on a tired radio,
And I won't tell no one your name.
And I won't tell 'em your name.

I think about you all the time,
But I don't need to sing.
It's lonely where you are.
Come back down and
I won't tell 'em your name.

1979

Words and Music by Billy Corgan

recorded by The Smashing Pumpkins

Shakedown nineteen seven-nine.
Cool kids never have the time.
On a live wire right up off the street;
You and I should meet.

Junebug skippin' like a stone
With the headlights pointed at the dawn.
We were sure we'd never see an end
To it all.

And I don't even care to shake these zipper blues.
And we don't know just where our bones will rest;
To dust, I guess.
Forgotten and absorbed into the earth below.

Double cross the vacant and the bored.
They're not sure just what we have in store.
Morphine city slippin' dues don't even care,
As restless as we are.

We feel the pull in the land of a thousand guilts.
And poured cement, lamented and assured
To the lights and towns below, faster than the speed of sound.
Faster than we thought we'd go, beneath the sound of hope.

Justine never knew the rules,
Hung down with the freaks and ghouls.
No apologies ever need be made.
I know you better than you fake it.

To see that we don't even care to shake these zipper blues.
And we don't know just where our bones will rest;
To dust, I guess.
Forgotten and absorbed into the earth below.

The street heats the urgency of now.
As you see there's no one around.

Nookie

Words and Music by Fred Durst, Wesley Borland, Sam Rivers, John Otto and
  Leor Dimant

recorded by Limp Bizkit

Spoken: Check, one, one, two.
I came into this world as a reject.
Look into these eyes, then you'll see the size of the flames.
Dwellin' on the past, (Past.) it's burnin' up my brain. (Hot.)
Everyone that burns has to learn from the pain.
Hey, I think about the day (Days.)
My girlie ran away with my pay when fellas came to (Play.) play.
Now she's stuck with my homies that she f***ed, (Ooh.)
And I'm just a sucker with a lump in my throat
(Hey.) like a chump, (Hey.) like a chump, (Hey.) like a chump, (Hey.)
Like a chump, (Hey.) like a chump, (Hey.) like a chump,
(Hey.) like a chump. (Hey.)

Should I be feelin' bad? (No.) Should I be feelin' good? (No.)
It's kinda sad, I'm the laughin' stock of the neighborhood.
And you would think that I'd be movin' on, (Movin'.)
But I'm a sucker like I said, f***-up in the head. (Not.)
Maybe she just made a mistake and I should give her a break.
My heart'll ache either way. Hey, what the hell.
What you want me to say? I won't lie, that I can't deny.

Refrain:
I did it all for the nookie, come on, the nookie, come on.
So you can take that cookie and stick it up your...Yeah!
Stick it up your...Yeah! Stick it up your...
I did it all for the nookie, come one, the nookie, come on.
So you can take that cookie and stick it up your...Yeah!
Stick it up your...Yeah! Stick it up your...Yeah!
Stick it up your...

Why did it take so long?
Why did I wait so long, huh, to figure it out?
But I didn't.
And I'm the only one underneath the sun who didn't get it.
I can't believe that I could be deceived (But you were.)
By my so-called girl, but in reality I had a hidden agenda.
She put my tender heart in a blender, and still I surrendered
(Hey.) like a chump, (Hey.) like a chump, (Hey.) like a chump, (Hey.)
Like a chump, (Hey.) like a chump, (Hey.) like a chump,
(Hey.) like a chump. (Hey.)

Refrain

Sung: I'm only human.
It's so easy for your friends to give you their advice.
They'll tell you just let it go. It's easier said than done.
I appreciate it. I do, but just leave me alone.
Leave me alone. Just leave me alone,
Ain't nothing gonna change, 'cause you can go away
And I'm just gonna stay here and always be the same.
Ain't nothing gonna change, 'cause you can go away
And I'm just gonna stay here and always be the same.
Ain't nothing gonna change, 'cause you can go away
And I'm just gonna stay here and always be the same.

Refrain

Only Happy When It Rains

Words and Music by Duke Erikson, Shirley Ann Manson, Steve Marker
  and Butch Vig

recorded by Garbage

I'm only happy when it rains.
I'm only happy when it's complicated.
And though I know you can't appreciate it,
I'm only happy when it rains.

You know I love it when the news is bad
And why it feels so good to feel so sad.
I'm only happy when it rains.

Pour your misery down,
Pour your misery down on me.
Pour your misery down,
Pour your misery down on me.

I'm only happy when it rains.
I feel good when things are goin' wrong.
I only listen to sad, sad songs.
I'm only happy when it rains.

I only smile in the dark.
My only comfort is the night gone black.
I didn't accidentally tell you that
I'm only happy when it rains.

You'll get the message by the time I'm through,
When I complain about me and you.
I'm only happy when it rains.

Pour your misery down,
Pour your misery down on me.
Pour your misery down,
Pour your misery down on me.

Pour your misery down,
Pour your misery down on me.
Pour your misery down.
You can keep me company
As long as you don't care
I'm only happy when it rains.

You'll wanna hear about my new obsession.
I'm riding high upon a deep depression.
I'm only happy when it rains.

Repeat and Fade:
Pour some misery down on me.
I'm only happy when it rains.

The Power of Love

Words by Mary Susan Applegate and Jennifer Rush
Music by Candy Derouge and Gunther Mende

recorded by Celine Dion

The whispers in the morning,
Of lovers sleeping tight,
Are rolling by like thunder now,
As I look into your eyes.

I hold on to your body,
And feel each move you make.
Your voice is warm and tender,
A love that I could not forsake.

Refrain:
'Cause I'm your lady
And you are my man.
Whenever you reach for me,
I'll do all that I can.

Even though there may be times
It seems I'm far away,
Never wonder where I am
'Cause I am always by your side.

Refrain

We're heading for something,
Somewhere I've never been.
Sometimes I am frightened
But I'm ready to learn
'Bout the power of love.

The sound of your heart beating
Made it clear and suddenly.
The feeling that I can't go on
Is light years away.

Refrain

We're heading for something,
Somewhere I've never been.
Sometimes I'm frightened
But I'm ready to learn
'Bout the power of love.
The power of love.

Pretty Fly (For a White Guy)

Words and Music by Dexter Holland

recorded by The Offspring

Spoken:
Oon-da glee-ben glauten glovin.
Give it to me, baby. Uh, huh, uh, huh.
Give it to me, baby. Uh, huh, uh, huh.
Give it to me, baby. Uh, huh, uh, huh.
And all the girlies say I'm pretty fly
For a white guy.
Uno, dos, tres, quatro cinco, cinco, seis.

Sung:
You know it's kind of hard just to get along today.
Our subject isn't cool but he fakes it anyway.
He may not have a clue and he may not have style,
But everything he lacks, well he makes up in denial.

Refrain:
So don't debate. He's a player straight.
You know he really doesn't get it anyway.
He's gonna play the field and keep it real.
For you no way, for you no way.
So if you don't rate, just overcompensate.
At least a you'll know you can always go on Rikki Lake.

The world needs wanna be's,
So hey, hey, do that brand new thing.

Give it to me, baby. Uh, huh, uh, huh.
Give it to me, baby. Uh, huh, uh, huh.
Give it to me, baby. Uh, huh, uh, huh.
And all the girlies say I'm pretty fly…
For a white guy.

Sung:
He needs some cool tunes, not just any will suffice.
But they didn't have Ice Cube so he bought Vanilla Ice.
Now cruising in his Pinto, he sees homies as he pass,
But if he looks twice, they're gonna kick his lily ass.

Refrain

The world needs wanna be's,
So hey, hey, do that brand new thing.

Now he's getting' a tattoo, yeah, he's gettin' ink done.
He asked for a thirteen but they drew a thirty-one.
Friends say he's trying too hard and he's not quite hip
But in his own mind he's the, he's the dopest trip.

Spoken:
Give it to me, baby. Uh, huh, uh, huh.
Give it to me, baby. Uh, huh, uh, huh.
Give it to me, baby. Uh, huh, uh, huh.
Uno, dos, tres, quatro cinco, cinco, seis.

Refrain

The world needs wanna be's, ah.
The world loves wanna be's, ah.
So let's get some more wanna be's
And hey, hey, do that brand new thing.

Ray of Light

Words and Music by William Orbit, Madonna, Clive Muldoon,
Dave Curtis and Christine Leach

recorded by Madonna

Zephyr in the sky at night,
I wonder do my tears of mourning sink beneath the sun?
She's got herself a universe gone quickly,
For the call of thunder threatens everyone.

And I feel like I just got home, and I feel.
And I feel like I just got home, and I feel.

Faster than the speeding light,
She's flying, trying to remember where it all began.
She's got herself a little piece of heaven,
Waiting for the time when earth shall be as one.

And I feel like I just got home, and I feel.
And I feel like I just got home, and I feel.

Quicker than a ray of light,
Quicker than a ray of light.

Zephyr in the sky at night,
I wonder do my tears of mourning sink beneath the sun?
She's got herself a universe gone quickly,
For the call of thunder threatens everyone.

And I feel like I just got home, and I feel.
And I feel like I just got home, and I feel.

Quicker than a ray of light,
Then gone for someone else shall be there
Through the endless years.

The Real Love

Words and Music by Bob Seger

recorded by Bob Seger

I think I've found the real love,
Genuine and true.
I think it's really come my way today, babe,
I think it's really you.

I remember moments looking in your eyes.
Could have sworn I saw the spark of love, babe,
Flickering inside.
I've been around and 'round this track,
And the only thing I lack is the real love.

Every time I see you, every time we touch,
I can feel the way you feel for me, babe,
And it means so much.
And every time you look at me,
It's just the way it all should be in the real love.

Oh, darlin', darlin', darlin',
Stay with me, stay.
I long to see you in the morning sun
Every day, every day.

So until that moment, when I take your hand,
I'm gonna try to do my very best, babe,
To prove that I'm your man.
I'm gonna do my very best,
I'm not gonna rest until we've got the real love.

Repeat and Fade:
Real love.
Until we've got the real love.

Right Here, Right Now

Words and Music by Jesus Jones

recorded by Jesus Jones

A woman on the radio talks about revolution
When it's already passed her by.
Bob Dylan denied this to sing about you know,
It feels good to be alive.

I was alive and I waited, waited.
I was alive and I waited for this.
Right here, right now
There is no other place I wanna be.
Right here, right now watching the world
Wake up from history.

Oh, I saw the decayin' when it seemed the world
Could change at the blink of an eye.
And if anything, then there's your sound of the times.

I was alive and I waited, waited.
I was alive and I waited for this.
Right here, right now.

I was alive and I waited, waited.
I was alive and I waited for this.
Right here, right now,
There is no other place I wanna be.
Right here, right now, watching the world
Wake up from history.

Right here, right now,
There is no other place I wanna be.
Right here, right now, watching the world
Wake up.

Run Around

Words and Music by John Popper

recorded by Blues Traveler

Oh, once upon a midnight, dearie,
I woke with something in my head.
I couldn't escape the memory of a phone call
And of what you said.

Like a game show contestant with a parting gift
I could not believe my eyes when I saw
Through the voice of a trusted friend
Who needs to humor me and tell me lies.
Yeah, humor me and tell me lies.

And I'll lie too and say I don't mind.
And as we seek, so shall we find.
And when you're feeling open I'll still be here,
But not without a certain degree of fear
Of what will be with you and me.
I still can see things, hopefully.

But you, why you wanna give me a run around?
Is it a surefire way to speed things up,
When all it does is slow me down?

And shake me and my confidence
'Bout a great many things,
But I've been there; I can see it cower
Like a nervous magician waiting in the wings.

Or a bad play where the heroes are right
And nobody thinks or expects too much,
And Hollywood's calling for the movie rights,
Singing, "Hey babe, keep in touch.
Hey baby, let's keep in touch."

But I want more than a touch.
I want you to reach me and show me
All the things no one else can see
So what you feel becomes mine as well,
And soon if we're lucky we'd be unable
To tell what's yours and mine.
The fishing's fine, and it doesn't have to rhyme
So don't you feed me a line.

But you, why you wanna give me a run around?
Is it a surefire way to speed things up,
When all it does is slow me down?

Tra la la bomba, dear, this is the pilot speaking
And I've got some news for you.
It seems my ship still stands no matter what you drop,
And there ain't a whole lot that you can do.

Oh sure, the banner may be torn and the wind's gotten colder.
Perhaps I've grown a little cynical.
But, I know no matter what the waitress brings,
I shall drink it and always be full.
Yeah, I will drink it and always be full.

Oh, I like coffee and I like tea.
But to be able to enter a final plea.
I still got this dream that you just can't shake.
I love you to the point you can no longer take.
Well, all right, okay, so be that way.
I hope and pray that there's something left to say.

But you, why you wanna give me a run around?
Is it a surefire way to speed things up,
When all it does is slow me down?

Oh, you. Why you wanna give me a run around?
Is it a surefire way to speed things up,
When all it does is slow me down?

Save the Best for Last

Words and Music by Phil Galdston, Jon Lind and Wendy Waldman

recorded by Vanessa Williams

Sometimes the snow comes down in June.
Sometimes the sun goes 'round the moon.
I see the passion in your eyes.
Sometimes it's all a big surprise.

'Cause there was a time when all I did
Was wish you'd tell me this was love.
It's not the way I hoped or how I planned,
But somehow it's enough.

And now we're standing face to face
Isn't this world a crazy place?
Just when I thought our chance had passed,
You go and save the best for last.

All of the nights you came to me
When some silly girl had set you free.
You wondered how you'd make it through.
I wondered what was wrong with you.

'Cause how could you give your love
To someone else and share your dreams with me?
Sometimes the very thing you're looking for
Is the one thing you can't see.

But now we're standing face to face,
Isn't this world a crazy place?
Just when I thought our chance had passed
You go and save the best for last.

Sometimes the very thing you're looking for
Is the one thing you can't see.

Sometimes the snow comes down in June.
Sometimes the sun goes 'round the moon.
Just when I thought a chance had passed,
You go and save the best for last.
You went and saved the best for last.

Semi-Charmed Life

Words and Music by Stephan Jenkins

recorded by Third Eye Blind

I'm packed and I'm holding.
I'm smiling, she's living, she's golden, she lives for me.
Says she lives for me.
Ovation, her own motivation.
She comes 'round and she goes down on me.
And I make her smile like a drug for you.
Do ever what you want to do.
Coming over you.
Keep on smiling what we go through.
One stop to the rhythm that divides you.
And I speak to you like the chorus to the verse.
Chop another line like a coda with a curse.
Come on like a freak show takes the stage.
We give them the games we play.
She said "I want something else
To get me through this semi-charmed life."
Baby, baby, I want something else.
I'm not listening when you say goodbye.

Do, do, do…
The sky, it was gold, it was rose.
I was taking sips of it through my nose.
And I wish I could get back there,
Someplace back there.
Smiling in the pictures you would take.
Doing crystal meth will lift you up until you break.
It won't stop. I won't come down,
I keep stock with a tick-tock rhythm.
A bump for the drop and then I bumped up,
I took the hit I was given then I bumped again,
Then I bumped again.
You said, "How do I get back there
To the place where I fell asleep inside you?"
How do I get myself back to the place where you said,
"I want something else
To get me through this semi-charmed life."
Baby, baby, I want something else.
I'm not listening when you say goodbye.

I believe in the sand beneath my toes.
The beach gives a feeling, an earthy feeling
I believe in the faith that grows.
And the four right chords and make me cry.
When I'm with you I feel like I could die
And that would be all right, all right.
And when the plane came in she said she was crashing.
The velvet, it rips.
In the city we tripped on the urge to feel alive.
But now I'm struggling to survive.
Those days you were wearing that velvet dress.
You're the priestess, I must confess.
Those little red panties, they pass the test.
Slide up around the belly, face down on the mattress.

One. And you hold me and we are broken.
Still, it's all that I want to do, just a little now.
Feel myself, head made of the ground.
I'm scared, I'm not coming down, no, no.
And I won't run for my life.
She's got her jaws just locked now in her smile
But nothing is right, all right.
And I want something else
To get me through this semi-charmed life.
Baby, I want something else,
Not listening when you say goodbye, goodbye.

The sky, it was gold, it was rose.
I was taking sips of it through my nose.
And I wish I could get back there,
Someplace back there in the place we used to stay.

She Don't Use Jelly

Words and Music by Wayne Coyne, Michael Ivins, Steven Drozd and Ronald Jones

recorded by The Flaming Lips

I know a girl who thinks it goes.
She'll make you breakfast, she'll make you toast.
But she don't use butter and she don't use cheese.
She don't use jelly or any of these.
She uses Vaseline, Vaseline, Vaseline.

I know a guy who goes to show.
When he's at home and, and he blows his nose,
He don't use tissues or his sleeve.
He don't use napkins or any of these.
He uses magazines, magazines, magazines.

I know a girl who reminds me of Cher.
She's always changing the color of her hair.
But she don't use nothin' that you buy at the store.
She likes her hair to be real orange.
She uses tangerines, tangerines, tangerines
Tangerines, tangerines, tangerines.

She's So High

Words and Music by Tal Bachman

recorded by Tal Bachman

She's blood, flesh and bone, no tucks or silicone.
She's touch, smell, sight, taste and sound.
But somehow I can't believe that anything should happen.

I know where I belong and nothin's gonna happen, yeah,
'Cause she's so high, high above me.
She's so lovely.
She's so high, like Cleopatra, Joan of Arc or Aphrodite.
Do, do, do, do, do. She's so high, high above me.

First class and fancy free, she's high society.
She's got the best of everything.
What could a guy like me ever really offer?

She's perfect as she can be.
Why should I even bother?
'Cause she's so high, high above me.
She's so lovely.
She's so high, like Cleopatra, Joan of Arc or Aphrodite.
Do, do, do, do, do. She's so high, high above me.

She calls to speak to me.
I freeze immediately 'cause what she says sounds so unreal.
'Cause somehow I can't believe that anything should happen.

I know where I belong and nothin's gonna happen, yeah,
'Cause she's so high, high above me.
She's so lovely.
She's so high, like Cleopatra, Joan of Arc or Aphrodite.
Oh, yeah. She's so high, high above me.

Strong Enough

Words and Music by Kevin Gilbert, David Baerwald, Sheryl Crow, Brian McLeod,
 Bill Bottrell and David Ricketts

recorded by Sheryl Crow

God I feel like hell tonight,
The tears of rage I cannot fight.
I'd be the last to help you understand.
Are you strong enough to be my man?
My man.

Nothing's true and nothing's right,
So let me be alone tonight.
You can't change the way I am.
Are you strong enough to be my man?

Refrain:
Lie to me, I promise I'll believe.
Lie to me, but please, don't leave.

I have a face I cannot show,
I make the rules up as I go.
It's try and love me if you can.
Are you man enough to be my man?
My man.

When I've shown you that I just don't care.
When I'm throwing punches in the air.
When I'm broken down and cannot stand.
Will you be strong enough to be my man?

Refrain

Silent Lucidity

Words and Music by Chris DeGarmo

recorded by Queensrÿche

Hush now, don't you cry.
Wipe away the teardrop from your eye.
You're lying, safe in bed;
It was all a bad dream spinning in your head

Your mind tricked you to feel the pain
Of someone close to you leaving the game of life.
So here it is, another chance, wide awake you face the day.
Your dream is over...or has it just begun?

There's a place I like to hide,
A doorway that I run through in the night.
Relax, child, you were there,
But only didn't realize and you were scared.

It's a place where you will learn
To face your fears, retrace the years
And ride the whims of your mind.
Commanding in another world,
Suddenly you hear and see this magic new dimension.

I will be watching over you.
I am gonna help to see you through.
I will protect you in the night.
I am smiling next to you in silent lucidity.

Spoken: Visualize your dreams.
Record it in the present tense.
Put it into a permanent form.
If you persist in your efforts,
You can achieve dream control...

Sung: If you open your mind for me,
You won't rely on open eyes to see.
The walls you built within come tumbling down
And a new world will begin.

Living twice at once you learn
You're safe from pain in the dream domain,
A soul set free to fly.

A round trip journey in your head,
Master of illusion,
Can you realize your dream's alive,
You can be the guide, but

I will be watching over you.
I am gonna help to see you through.
I will protect you in the night.
I am smiling next to you.

Smells Like Teen Spirit

Words and Music by Kurt Cobain, Krist Novoselic and Dave Grohl

recorded by Nirvana

Load up on guns, bring your friends.
It's fun to lose and to pretend.
She's overboard, self assured.
Oh, no, I know a dirty word.

Hello, hello, hello. How low?
Hello, hello, hello. How low?
Hello, hello, hello. How low?
Hello, hello, hello.

With the lights out it's less dang'rous.
Here we are now; entertain us.
I feel stupid and contagious.
Here we are now; entertain us.

A mulatto, an albino,
A mosquito, my libido.
Yeah!
Oy. Oy.

I'm worse at what I do best,
And for this gift I feel blessed.
Our little trap has always been
And always will until the end.

Hello, hello, hello. How low?
Hello, hello, hello. How low?
Hello, hello, hello. How low?
Hello, hello, hello.

With the lights out it's less dang'rous.
Here we are now; entertain us.
I feel stupid and contagious.
Here we are now; entertain us.

A mulatto, an albino,
A mosquito, my libido.
Yeah!
Oy. Oy.

And I forget just why I taste.
Oh, yeah, I guess it makes me smile.
I found it hard; it was hard to find.
Oh, well, whatever, never mind.

Hello, hello, hello. How low?
Hello, hello, hello. How low?
Hello, hello, hello. How low?
Hello, hello, hello.

With the lights out it's less dang'rous.
Here we are now; entertain us.
I feel stupid and contagious.
Here we are now; entertain us.

A mulatto, an albino,
A mosquito, my libido.
A denial, a denial.
A denial, a denial.
A denial, a denial.
A denial, a denial.

Smooth

Words by Rob Thomas
Music by Rob Thomas and Itaal Shur

recorded by Santana featuring Rob Thomas

Man, it's a hot one.
Like seven inches from the midday sun.
Well, I hear your whisper and the words melt everyone.
But you stay so cool.
My Munequita, my Spanish Harlem Mona Lisa.
Well, you're my reason for reason, the step in my groove.

And if you said this life ain't good enough,
I would give my world to lift you up,
I could change my life to better suit your mood.
'Cause you're so smooth.

And it's just like the ocean under the moon.
Well, it's the same as the emotion that I get from you.
You got the kind of livin' that can be so smooth,
'Give me your heart. Make it real or else forget about it.

Well, I'll tell you one thing,
If you would leave it'd be a crying shame.
In every breath and every word I hear your name calling me out.
Out from the barrio, you hear my rhythm on your radio.
You feel the turning of the world so soft and slow;
Turning me round and round.

And if you said this life ain't good enough,
I would give my world to lift you up,
I could change my life to better suit your mood.
'Cause you're so smooth.

And it's just like the ocean under the moon.
Well, it's the same as the emotion that I get from you.
You got the kind of livin' that can be so smooth,
'Give me your heart. Make it real or else forget about it.

And it's just like the ocean under the moon.
Well, it's the same as the emotion that I get from you.
You got the kind of livin' that can be so smooth,
'Give me your heart. Make it real or else forget about it.

Spoken: Or else forget about it.
Or else forget about it.
Let's don't forget about it.
Sung: Give me your heart, make it real.
Let's don't forget about it

Repeat and Fade:
Let's don't forget about it.

Stay

Words and Music by Lisa Loeb

recorded by Lisa Loeb & Nine Stories

You say I only hear what I want to.
You say I talk so all the time. So?
And I thought what I felt was simple.
And I thought that I don't belong.
And now that I am leavin'
Now I know that I did something wrong.
'Cause I missed you, yeah, yeah, I missed you.

And you say I only hear what I want to.
I don't listen hard, I don't pay attention
To the distance that you're running,
Or to anyone, anywhere.
I don't understand if you really care.
I'm only hearing negatives, no, no, no.

So I turned the radio on. I turned the radio up.
And this woman was singin' my song.
Lovers in love and the others run away.
The lover is cryin' 'cause the other won't stay.
Some of us hover when we weep for the other
Who was dyin' since the day they were born,
Well, this is not that.

I think I am throwin', but I'm thrown.
And I thought I'd live forever,
But now I'm not so sure.
You try to tell me that I'm clever,
But that won't take me anyhow,
Or anywhere with you.

And you said that I was naïve
And I thought that I was strong.
I thought, "Hey, I can leave, I can leave, oh."
But now I know that I was wrong
'Cause I missed you, yeah, missed you.

You said you caught me 'cause you want me
And one day you'll let me go.
You try to give away a keeper, or keep me
'Cause you know you're just too scared to lose.
And you say, 'Stay.'
You say I only hear what I want to.

Superstar

Written by Lauryn Hill
With Additional Lyrical Contribution by Johari Newton and
  Additional Musical Contribution by James Poyser

recorded by Lauryn Hill

Spoken:
Yo, hip-hop started out in the heart, uh-huh, yo.
Now everybody tryin' to chart. Say what?
Hip-hop started out in the heart, yo, uh.
Now everybody tryin' to chart.
C'mon now, baby. C'mon now, baby.
C'mon now, baby. C'mon. Woo.
C'mon now, baby. C'mon now, baby.
C'mon now, baby, c'mon.

Refrain, sung:
Come on, baby, light my fire.
Everything you drop is so tired.
Music is supposed to inspire.
How come we ain't getting no higher?

Now tell me your philosophy
On exactly what an artist should be.
Should they be someone with prosperity
And no concept of reality?
Now who you know without any flaws
That live above the spiritual laws?
And does anything they feel just because
There's always someone there who'll applaud. Yeah.

Refrain

I know you think that you've got it all.
And by making other people feel small
Makes you think you're unable to fall.
But when you do who you gonna call?
See what you give is just what you get.
I know it hasn't hit you yet.
Now, I don't mean to get you upset,
But every cause has an effect. Uh huh.

Refrain

Rap:
I cross sands in distant lands, make plans with the sheiks.
Why you beef with freaks as my album sales peak?
All I wanted was to sell like 500
And be a ghetto superstar since my first album, *Blunted*.
I used to work at Foot Locker, they fired me and fronted.
Or I quitted, now I spit it—however do you want it?
Now you get it!
Writing rhymes my range with the frames slightly tinted.
Then send it to your block and have my full name cemented.
And if your rhymes sound like mine, I'm taking a percentage.
Unprecedented and still respected when it vintage.
I'm serious, I'm taking over areas in Aquarius.
Running red lights with my 10,000 chariots.
Just as Christ was a superstar, you stupid star.
They'll hail you then they'll nail you, no matter who you are.
They'll make you now then take you down.
And make you face it, if you slit the bag open.
And put your pinky in it, then taste it.

Refrain Three Times

Tears in Heaven

Words and Music by Eric Clapton and Will Jennings

recorded by Eric Clapton

Would you know my name
If I saw you in heaven?
Would it be the same
If I saw you in heaven?
I must be strong and carry on,
'Cause I know I don't belong
Here in heaven.

Would you hold my hand
If I saw you in heaven?
Would you help me stand
If I saw you in heaven?
I'll find my way through night and day,
'Cause I know I just can't stay
Here in heaven.

Time can bring you down,
Time can bend your knees.
Time can break your heart,
Have you beggin' please, beggin' please.

Beyond the door
There's peace, I'm sure,
And I know there'll be no more
Tears in heaven.

Repeat Verse 1

Til I Hear It from You

Words and Music by Jesse Valenzuela, Robin Wilson and Marshall Crenshaw

recorded by Gin Blossoms

I didn't ask, they shouldn't have told me.
At first I'd laugh, but now
It's sinkin' in fast, whatever they sold me.
But baby, I don't wanna take advice from fools.
I'll just figure everything is cool
Until I hear it from you. (Hear it from you.)

It gets hard when memory's faded is what they say.
It's likely they're just jealous and jaded.
But maybe I don't wanna take advice from fools.
I'll just figure everything is cool
Until I hear it from you. (Hear it from you.)

I can't let it get me off,
Or break up my train of thought.
As far as I know, nothin's wrong
Until I hear it from you.

Still thinking about not living without it,
Outside, lookin' in til we're talkin' about not steppin' around it.
But lately I don't wanna take advice from fools.
I just take it everything is cool
Until I hear it from you. (Hear it from you.)
Until I hear it from you. (Hear it from you.)
Til I hear it from you, oh, no.

Repeat and Fade:
Til I hear it from you.
(Don't take advice from fools,
And figure everything is cool.)
Til I hear it from you.

That Thing You Do!

Words and Music by Adam Schlesinger

from the Original Motion Picture Soundtrack *That Thing You Do!*
recorded by The Wonders

You, doin' that thing you do,
Breaking my heart in to a million pieces
Like you always do.
And you don't mean to be cruel.
You'd never even knew about the heartache
I've been going through.
Well, I try and try to forget you, girl,
But it's just so hard to do
Every time you do that thing you do.

I know all the games you play,
And I'm gonna find a way to let you know that
You'll be mine someday
'Cause we could be happy, can't you see,
If you'd only let me be the one to hold you
And keep you here with me.
'Cause I try and try to forget you, girl,
But it's just so hard to do
Every time you do that thing you do.

I don't ask a lot, girl,
But I know one thing's for sure.
It's the love I haven't got, girl,
And I just can't take it anymore. Whoa.

'Cause we could be happy, can't you see,
If you'd only let me be the one to hold you
And keep you here with me.
'Cause it hurts me so just to see you go
Around with someone new,
And if I know you, you're doin' that thing,
Every day just doin' that thing.
I can't take you doin' that thing you do.

This Kiss

Words and Music by Annie Roboff, Beth Nielsen Chapman and Robin Lerner

recorded by Faith Hill

I don't want another heartbreak.
I don't need another turn to cry, no.
I don't want to learn the hard way.
Baby, hello, oh no, goodbye.
But you got me like a rocket
Shooting straight across the sky.

It's the way you love me. It's a feeling like this.
It's centrifugal motion. It's perpetual bliss.
It's that pivotal moment. It's ah, impossible.
This kiss, this kiss, unstoppable. This kiss, this kiss.

Cinderella said to Snow White,
"How does love get so off course?" Oh.
All I wanted was a white knight
With a good heart, soft touch, fast horse.
Ride me off into the sunset,
Baby, I'm forever yours.

It's the way you love me. It's a feeling like this.
It's centrifugal motion. It's perpetual bliss.
It's that pivotal moment. It's ah, unthinkable.
This kiss, this kiss, unsinkable. This kiss, this kiss.

You can kiss me in the moonlight,
On the rooftop, under the sky, oh.
You can kiss me with the windows
Open while the rain comes blowin' inside, oh.
Kiss me in sweet, slow motion.
Let's let everything slide.
You got me floating, you got me flying.

Repeat and Fade:
It's the way you love me. It's a feeling like this.
It's centrifugal motion. It's perpetual bliss.
It's that pivotal moment. It's ah, subliminal.
This kiss, this kiss, it's criminal.
This kiss, this kiss.
It's the way you love me, baby.
It's the way you love me, darling.

Torn

Words and Music by Phil Thornalley, Scott Cutler and Anne Previn

recorded by Natalie Imbruglia

I thought I saw a man brought to life.
He was warm, he came around
Like he was dignified.
He showed me what it was to cry.
Well, you couldn't be that man I adored.
You don't seem to know or seem to care
What your heart is for.
Well, I don't know him anymore.
There's nothing where he used to lie.
My conversation has run dry.
That's what's going on.
Nothing's fine,

Refrain:
I'm torn.
I'm all out of faith,
This is how I feel.
I'm cold and I am shamed
Lying naked on the floor.
Illusion never changed into something real.
I'm wide awake
And I can see the perfect sky is torn.
You're a little late.
I'm already torn.

So, I guess the fortune teller's right.
I should've seen just what was there
And not some holy light.
But you crawled beneath my veins, and now
I don't care,
I have no luck.
I don't miss it all that much.
There's just so many things
That I can't touch.

Refrain

Torn.
Ooh, ooh.
There's nothing where he used to lie.
My inspiration has run dry.
That's what's going on.
Nothing's right,

Refrain

I'm all out of faith,
This is how I feel.
I'm cold and I'm bound and broken on the floor.
You're a little late.
I'm already torn.
Torn.

Truly, Madly, Deeply

Words and Music by Daniel Jones and Darren Hayes

recorded by Savage Garden

I'll be your dream, I'll be your wish,
I'll be your fantasy.
I'll be your hope,
I'll be your love
Be everything that you need.
I'll love you more with every breath,
Truly, madly, deeply do.
I will be strong, I will be faithful,
'Cause I'm counting on a new beginning.
A reason for living,
A deeper meaning, yeah.

Refrain:
I want to stand with you on a mountain,
I want to bathe with you in the sea.
I want to lay like this forever,
Until the sky falls down on me.

And then the stars are shining brightly
In the velvet sky,
I'll make a wish and send it to heaven,
Then make you want to cry
The tears of joy
For all the pleasure in the certainty,
That we're surrounded by the comfort
And protection of the highest powers,
In lonely hours,
The tears devour you.

Refrain

Oh, can you see it baby?
You don't have to close your eyes
'Cause it's standing right beside you, ooh.
All that you need will surely come.

Repeat Verse 1 and Refrain

Under the Bridge

Words and Music by Anthony Kiedis, Flea, John Frusciante and Chad Smith

recorded by Red Hot Chili Peppers

Sometimes I feel like I don't have a partner.
Sometimes I feel like my only friend
Is the city I live in, the city of angels.
Lonely as I am, together we cry.

I drive on her streets 'cause she's my companion.
I walk through her hills 'cause she knows who I am.
She sees my good deeds and she kisses me windy.
I never worry. Now, that is a lie.

Refrain:
I don't ever want to feel like I did that day.
Take me to the place I love, take me all the way.
I don't ever want to feel like I did that day.
Take me to the place I love, take me all the way,
Yeah, yeah, yeah.

It's hard to believe that there's nobody out there.
It's hard to believe that I'm all alone.
At least I have her love, the city, she loves me.
Lonely as I am, together we cry.

Refrain

Oh, no no no, yeah, yeah.
Love me, I said, yeah, yeah.
Spoken: One time.

Sung:
Under the bridge downtown is where I drew some blood.
Under the bridge downtown I could not get enough.
Under the bridge downtown forgot about my love.
Under the bridge downtown I gave my life away.

Unskinny Bop

Words and Music by Bobby Dall, Brett Michaels, Bruce Johannesson and
  Rikki Rockett

recorded by Poison

Oh, what's got you so jumpy?
Why can't you sit still, yeah?
Like gasoline you want to pump me
And leave me when you get your fill, yeah.

Every time I touch you, you get hot,
I want to make love, you never stop.
Come up for air, pull me to the floor.
Just what's been going on in that head of yours?

Refrain:
Unskinny bop just blows me away.
Yeah, unskinny bop, bop, all night and day, yeah.
Unskinny bop, bop, bop, bop, she just loves to play.
Unskinny bop, nothin' more to say.

You look at me so funny.
Love bite got you acting oh so strange.
You got too many bees in your honey
Am I just another word in your page, yeah.

Every time I touch you, you get hot,
I want to make love, you never stop.
Come up for air, pull me to the floor.
Just what's been going on in that head of yours?

Refrain

You're saying my love won't do ya.
That ain't love, written on your face.
Well, honey, I can see right through ya.
We'll see who's ridin' who at the end of the race.

What's right? What's wrong?
What's left? What the hell is going on?

Refrain

Spoken: Come up for air, pull me to the floor.

Walking in Memphis

Words and Music by Marc Cohn

recorded by Marc Cohn

Put on my blue suede shoes
And I boarded the plane.
Touched down in the land of the Delta Blues
In the middle of the pouring rain.
W.C. Handy—won't you look down over me?
Yeah, I got a first class ticket,
But I'm as blue as a boy can be.

Then I'm walking in Memphis,
Was walking with my feet ten feet off ofBeale.
Walking in Memphis,
But do I really feel the way I feel?

Saw the ghost of Elvis
On Union Avenue.
Followed him up to the gates of Graceland,
Then I watched him walk right through.
Now security they did not see him,
They just hovered 'round his tomb.
But there's a pretty little thing
Waiting for the King
Down in the Jungle Room.

When I was walking in Memphis,
I was walking with my feet ten feet off of Beale.
Walking in Memphis,
But do I really feel the way I feel?

They've got catfish on the table.
They've got gospel in the air.
And Reverend Green be glad to see you
When you haven't got a prayer.
But, boy, you've got a prayer in Memphis.

Now Muriel plays piano
Every Friday at The Hollywood.
And they brought me down to see her.
And they asked me if I would
Do a little number,
And I sang with all my might.
She said, "Tell me, are you a Christian child?"
And I said, "Ma'am, I am tonight."

Walking in Memphis,
Was walking with my feet ten feet off of Beale.
Walking in Memphis,
But do I really feel the way I feel?

Walking in Memphis,
I was walking with my feet ten feet off of Beale.
Walking in Memphis,
But do I really feel the way I feel?

Put on my blue suede shoes
And I boarded the plane.
Touched down in the land of the Delta Blues
In the middle of the pouring rain.
Touched down in the land of the Delta Blues
In the middle of the pouring rain.

Walking on Broken Glass

Words and Music by Annie Lennox

recorded by Annie Lennox

Walking on, walking on broken glass.
Walking on, walking on broken glass.

You were the sweetest thing that I ever knew,
But I don't care for sugar, honey, if I can't have you.
Since you abandoned me, my whole life has crashed.
Won't you pick the pieces up
'Cause it feels just like I'm walking on broken glass.
Walking on, walking on broken glass.
Whoo, hoo, yeah. Walking on, walking on broken glass.

The sun's still shining in the deep blue sky,
But it don't mean nothing to me.
Whoa, let the rain come down,
Let the wind blow through me.
I'm living in an empty room
With all the windows smashed,
And I've got so little left to lose
That it feels just like I'm walking on broken glass.
Walking on, walking on broken glass.

And if you're trying to cut me down,
You know that I might leave
'Cause if you try to cut me down,
I know that you'll succeed.
And if you want to hurt me,
There's nothing left to fear
'Cause if you want to hurt me,
You're doing really well by me.

Now every one of us is made to suffer,
Every one of us is made to weep,
But we've been hurting one another.
Now the pain has cut too deep.
So, take me from the wreckage,
Save me from the blast.
Lift me up and take me back.
Don't let me keep on walking.
I can't keep on walking on,
I can't keep on walking on broken glass.
Walking on, walking on broken glass.

Repeat and Fade:
Walking on, walking on broken glass.

Waterfalls

Words and Music by Marqueze Etheridge, Lisa Nicole Lopes, Rico R. Wade,
    Pat Brown and Ramon Murray

recorded by TLC

A lonely mother gazing out of her window
Staring at a son she just can't touch.
If at any time he's in a jam she'll be by his side,
But he doesn't realize he hurts her so much.
But all the praying just ain't helping at all,
'Cause he can't seem to keep his self out of trouble.
So, he goes out and he makes his money
The best way he knows how,
Another body laying cold in the gutter.
Listen to me.

Refrain:
Don't go chasing waterfalls.
Please stick to the rivers and the lakes that you're used to.
I know that you're gonna have it your way or nothing at all,
But I think you're moving too fast.

Little precious has a natural obsession
For temptation, but he just can't see.
She gives him loving that his body can't handle,
But all he can say is, "Baby, it's so good to me."
One day he goes and takes a glimpse in the mirror,
But he doesn't recognize his won face.
His health is fading and doesn't know why.
Three letters took him to his final resting place.
Y'all don't hear me.

Refrain

Rap:
I seen a rainbow yesterday
But too many storms have come and gone
Leavin' a trace of not one God-given ray
Is it because my life is ten shades of gray
I pray all ten fade away.
Seldom praise Him for the sunny days
And like His promises true
Only my faith can undo
The many chances I blew.
To bring my life to a new
Clear blue and unconditional skies
Have dried the tears from my eyes.
No more lonely cries
My only bleedin' hope
Is for the folk who can't cope
Wit such an endurin' pain
That it keeps 'em in the pourin' rain.
Who's to blame
For tootin' caine in your own vein.
What a shame
You shoot and aim for someone else's brain.
You claim the insane
Name this day in time
For fallin' prey to crime.
I say the system got you victim to your own mind.
Dreams are hopeless aspirations
In hopes of comin' true.
Believe in yourself.
The rest is up to me and you.

Refrain

What I Got

Words and Music by Brad Nowell, Eric Wilson, Floyd Gaugh and Lindon Roberts

recorded by Sublime

Early in the mornin', risin' to the street.
Light me up that cigarette and I strap shoes on my feet.
(De, de, de, de de.)
Got to find a reason, reason things went wrong.
Got to find a reason why my money's all gone.
I got a Dalmation, and I can still get high.
I can play the guitar like a mother fuckin' riot.

Well, life is too short so love the one you got
'Cause you might get run over or you might get shot.
Never start no static, I just get it off my chest.
Never has to battle with no bulletproof vest.
Take a small example, take a ti-ti-ti-tip from me.
Take all of your money, give it all…

Love is what I got, it's within my reach
And the sublime style's still straight from Long Beach.
It all comes back to you, you finally get what you deserve.
Try and test that, you're bound to get served.
Love's what I got, don't start a riot.
You feel it when the dance gets hot.

Refrain:
Lovin' is what I got. I said remember that.
Lovin' is what I got, and remember that.
Lovin' is what I got. I said remember that.
Lovin' is what I got, I got, I got, I got.

Why, I don't cry when my dog runs away.
I don't get angry at the bills I have to pay.
I don't get angry when my mom smokes pot,
Hits the bottle and moves right to the rock.
Fuckin' and fightin', it's all the same.
Livin' with Louie Dog's the only way to stay sane.
Let the lovin', let the lovin' come back to me.

Refrain

Whatever

Words and Music by Sully Erna and Tony Rombola

recorded by Godsmack

And I wonder day to day. I don't like you anyway.
I don't need your shit today.You're pathetic in your own way.
I feel for you. (Better fuckin' go away.)
I will behave. Better fuckin' go away.

I'm doing the best I ever did.
I'm doing the best that I can.
I'm doing the best I ever did, uh, aw.

I don't need to fantasize, you are my pets all the time.
I don't mind if you go blind.
You get what you get until you're through with my life.
I feel for you. (Better fuckin' go away.)
I will behave. You better go away.
I feel for you. (Better fuckin' go away.)
I will behave. You better go away.

I'm doing the best I ever did.
I'm doing the best that I can.
I'm doing the best I ever did, now go away.
I'm doing the best I ever did.
I'm doing the best that I can.
I'm doing the best I ever did, now go away.

I'm doing the best I ever did. (Go away.)
I'm doing the best that I can. (Go away.)
I'm doing the best I ever did. (Go away.)
I'm doing the best that I can. (Go away.)

I'm doing the best I ever did.
I'm doing the best that I can.
I'm doing the best I ever did, now go away.
I'm doing the best I ever did.
I'm doing the best that I can.
I'm doing the best I ever did, now go away.

Yeah. Yeah. Yeah. Yeah.
Yeah. Yeah. Yeah. Yeah.
I'm doing the best that I ever did. (Go away.)
I'm doing the best that I can.

When You Say Nothing at All

Words and Music by Don Schlitz and Paul Overstreet

recorded by Alison Krauss & Union Station

It's amazing how you can speak right to my heart.
Without saying a word you can light up the dark.
Try as I may I could never explain
What I hear when you don't say a thing.

Refrain:
The smile on your face lets me know that you need me.
There's truth in your eyes saying you'll never leave me.
A touch of your hand says you'll catch me if ever I fall.
Now you say it's best when you say nothing at all.

All day long I can hear people talking out loud,
But when you hold me near you drown out the crowd.
Old Mister Webster could never define
What's being said between your heart and mine.

Refrain

Zombie

Lyrics and Music by Dolores O'Riordan

recorded by The Cranberries

Another head hangs lowly, child is slowly taken.
And the violence caused such silence,
Who are the mistaken?
But you see, it's not me, it's not my family.
It's in your head, in your head they are fighting
With their tanks, and their bombs and their bombs and their guns.
In your head, in your head they are crying,
In your head, in your head, zombie, zombie, zombie, hey, hey.
What's in your head, in your head, zombie, zombie, zombie?
Hey, hey, hey, oh, doo, doo, doo, doo, doo, doo, doo, doo,
Doo, doo , doo, doo, doo, doo, doo, doo.

Another mother's breakin' heart is taking over.
When the violence causes silence, we must be mistaken.
It's the same old theme since nineteen-sixteen.
It's in your head, in your head they're still fighting
With their tanks, and their bombs and their bombs and their guns.
In your head, in your head they are dying,
In your head, in your head, zombie, zombie, zombie, hey, hey.
What's in your head, in your head, zombie, zombie, zombie?
Hey, hey, hey, oh, oh, oh, oh, oh, oh, oh, hey, oh, ya, ya.

Wonderwall

Words and Music by Noel Gallagher

recorded by Oasis

Today is gonna be the day
That they're gonna throw it back to you.
By now you should have somehow realized
What you gotta do.
I don't believe that anybody feels
The way I do about you now.

Backbeat, the word is on the street
That the fire in your heart is out.
I'm sure you've heard it all before,
But you never really had a doubt.
I don't believe that anybody feels
The way I do about you now.

And all the roads we have to walk are winding,
And all the lights that lead us there are blinding.
There are many things that I would like to say to you,
But I don't know how.
Because maybe you're gonna be the one that saves me.
And after all you're my wonderwall.

Today was gonna be the day,
But they'll never throw it back to you.
By now you should have somehow realized
What you're not to do.
I don't believe that anybody feels
The way I do about you now.
And all the roads that lead you there were winding,
And all the lights that light the way are blinding.
There are many things that I would like to say to you,
But I don't know how.

Three Times:
I said maybe you're gonna be the one that saves me.
And after all you're my wonderwall.

I said maybe (I said maybe).
You're gonna be the one that saves me.
(Saves me.)
You're gonna be the one that saves me.

You Oughta Know

Lyrics by Alanis Morissette
Music by Alanis Morissette and Glen Ballard

recorded by Alanis Morissette

I want you to know that I'm happy for you.
I wish nothing but the best for you both.
An older version of me, is she perverted like me?
Would she go down on you in a theater?
Does she speak eloquently, and would she have your baby?
I'm sure she'd make a really excellent mother.

'Cause the love that you gave that we made wasn't able to
Make it enough for you to be open wide, no.
And every time you speak her name does she know
How you told me you'd hold me until you died, till you died?
But you're still alive.

Refrain:
And I'm here to remind you
Of the mess you left when you went away.
It's not fair to deny me
Of the cross I bear that you gave to me.
You, you, you oughta know.

You seem very well, things look peaceful.
I'm not quite as well, I thought you should know.
Did you forget about me, Mister Duplicity?
I hate to bug you in the middle of dinner.
It was a slap in the face, how quickly I was replaced,
And are you thinking of me when you fuck her?

'Cause the love that you gave that we made wasn't able to
Make it enough for you to be open wide, no.
And every time you speak her name does she know
How you told me you'd hold me until you died, till you died?
But you're still alive.

Refrain

'Cause the joke that you laid in the bed that was me and I'm
Not gonna fade as soon as you close your eyes, and you know it.
And every time I scratch my nails down someone else's back,
I hope you feel it. Well, can you feel it?

Refrain Twice

You Were Meant for Me

Lyrics by Jewel Kilcher
Music by Jewel Kilcher and Steve Poltz

recorded by Jewel

I hear the clock. It's six A.M.
I feel so far from where I've been.
I got my eggs, I got my pancakes, too.
I got my maple syrup, everything but you.
I break the yolks and make a smiley face.
I kinda like it in my brand new place.
Wipe the spots up over me,
Don't leave my keys in the door.
I never put wet towels on the floor anymore

Refrain:
'Cause dreams last so long,
Even after you're gone.
I know that you love me,
And soon you will see,
You were meant for me,
And I was meant for you.

I called my mama, she was out for a walk.
Consoled a cup of coffee, but I didn't want to talk.
So, I picked up the paper, it was more bad news.
My heart's being broken by people being used.
Put on my coat in the pouring rain.
I saw a movie, it just wasn't the same

Refrain

I go about my business. I'm doing fine.
Besides what would I say if I had you on the line?
Same old story, not much to say.
Hearts are broken every day.

I brush my teeth, I put the cap back on.
I know you hate it when I leave the light on.
I pick up a cup and then I turn the sheets down
And then I take a deep breath, a good look around.
Put on my pj's and hop into bed.
I'm half alive, but I feel mostly dead.
I try and tell myself it'll be alright.
I just shouldn't think anymore tonight.

Refrain

Yeah, you were meant for me and I was meant for you.

You'll Be in My Heart (Pop Version)

Words and Music by Phil Collins

from Walt Disney Pictures' *Tarzan*™
recorded by Phil Collins

Come, stop your crying; it will be all right.
Just take my hand, hold it tight.
I will protect you from all around you.
I will be here; don't you cry.

For one so small, you seem so strong.
My arms will hold you, keep you
safe and warm.
This bond between us can't be broken.
I will be here; don't you cry.

Refrain:
'Cause you'll be in my heart,
Yes, you'll be in my heart,
From this day on, now and forever more.
You'll be in my heart,
No matter what they say.
You'll be here in my heart always.

Why can't they understand the way we feel?
They just don't trust what they can't explain.
I know we're different, but deep inside us,
We're not that different at all.
And...

Refrain

Don't listen to them,
'Cause what do they know?
We need each other to have, to hold.
They'll see in time,
I know.

When destiny calls you,
You must be strong.
It may not be with you,
But you've got to hold on.
They'll see in time, I know.
We'll show them together,

'Cause you'll be in my heart.
Believe me, you'll be in my heart.
I'll be there from this day on,
Now and forevermore.

You'll be in my heart,
(You'll be here in my heart.)
No matter what they say.
(I'll be with you.)
You'll be here in my heart,
(I'll be there.)
Always.

I'll be with you.
I'll be there for you, always,
Always and always.
Just look over your shoulder.
Just look over your shoulder.
Just look over you shoulder;
I'll be there always.

You're Still the One

Words and Music by Shania Twain and Robert John Lange

recorded by Shania Twain

When I first saw you, I saw love.
And the first time you touched me, I felt love.
And after all this time, you're still the one I love.

Looks like we made it.
Look how far we've come, my baby.
We might-a took the long way.
We knew we'd get there someday.

They said, "I bet they'll never make it."
But just look at us holding on.
We're still together, still going strong.
(You're still the one.)
You're still the one I run to,
The one that I belong to.
You're still the one I want for life.
(You're still the one.)
You're still the one that I love,
The only one I dream of.
You're still the one I kiss good night.

Ain't nothin' better,
We beat the odds together.
I'm glad we didn't listen.
Look at what we would be missing.

They said, "I bet they'll never make it."
But just look at us holding on.
We're still together, still going strong.
(You're still the one.)
You're still the one I run to,
The one that I belong to.
You're still the one I want for life.
(You're still the one.)
You're still the one that I love,
The only one I dream of.
You're still the one I kiss good night.
You're still the one.

You're still the one I run to,
The one that I belong to.
You're still the one I want for life.
(You're still the one.)
You're still the one that I love,
The only one I dream of.
You're still the one I kiss good night.
I'm so glad we made it.
Look how far we've come, my baby.